Say It Right

A Guide to Effective
Oral Business Presentations

D0080054

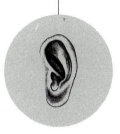

Say It Right
A Guide to Effective
Oral Business Presentations

Garth A. Hanson

Kaye T. Hanson

Ted D. Stoddard

All of Management Communication Department
Brigham Young University

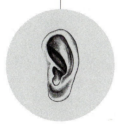

IRWIN

Chicago • Bogotá • Boston • Buenos Aires • Caracas
London • Madrid • Mexico City • Sydney • Toronto

IRWIN

Concerned About Our Environment

In recognition of the fact that our company is a large end-user of fragile yet replenishable resources, we at Irwin can assure you that every effort is made to meet or exceed Environmental Protection Agency (EPA) recommendations and requirements for a "greener" workplace. To preserve these natural assets, a number of environmental policies, both companywide and department-specific, have been implemented. From the use of 50% recycled paper in our textbooks to the printing of promotional materials with recycled stock and soy inks to our office paper recycling program, we are committed to reducing waste and replacing environmentally unsafe products with safer alternatives.

© Richard D. Irwin, Inc., 1995

All rights reserved. No part of this publication may be reproduced, stored in a retrieval system, or transmitted in any form or by any means, electronic, mechanical, photocopying, recording, or otherwise, without the prior written permission of the publisher.

Senior sponsoring editor:	Craig Beytien
Editorial assistant:	Jennifer R. McBride
Senior marketing manager:	Kurt Messersmith
Project editor:	Beth Yates
Production manager:	Pat Frederickson
Cover design:	a.m. Design
Art manager:	Kim Meriwether
Interior design and compositing:	Rock, Paper, Scissors
Typeface:	ITC Berkeley Oldstyle
Printer:	R.R. Donnelley and Sons Company

Library of Congress Cataloging-in-Publication Data

Hanson, Garth A.
    Say it right: a guide to effective oral business presentations
  Garth A. Hanson, Kaye T. Hanson, Ted D. Stoddard.
      p. cm.
    ISBN 0-256-14546-6
    1. Business presentations. I. Hanson, Kaye T. II. Stoddard, Ted D. III. Title.
  HF5718.22.H36 1995
  658.4'52—dc20   94—26273

Printed in the United States of America
1 2 3 4 5 6 7 8 9 0 DO 1 0 9 8 7 6 5 4

Preface SAY IT RIGHT

Say It Right: A Guide to Effective Oral Business Presentations contains tried and proven techniques for giving oral presentations. The book reflects the collective efforts of three professors of management communication who have devoted their careers to written and oral communication in the business world and the business classroom.

Our goal has been to prepare a book to help both practicing business executives and classroom business students prepare and deliver outstanding oral presentations. Throughout our careers, we have practiced the book's techniques in giving countless business presentations and in teaching both undergraduate and graduate management communication courses. The techniques we espouse work! We have perfected them, and we present them to you in a simple, easy-to-understand approach.

Say It Right has four parts:

- Getting Ready
- Developing the Presentation
- Delivering the Presentation
- Cleaning Up Loose Ends

Parts II and III contain the primary directives and procedures for developing and delivering effective oral presentations.

A distinctive feature of Part II of *Say It Right* is the unique planning tool we call *The FourMat.* * Once you have mastered the simple steps for using *The FourMat,* you will appreciate its flexibility in helping you develop and deliver any presentation. We think you will use *The FourMat* throughout your career when you develop and deliver short, medium, or long presentations for any purpose and for any audience. Its simplicity will delight you and keep you from jumping

---

* Adapted from the Four-Box method in *Effective Business Writing,* published by Shipley Associates, ©1988. Used with permission of Franklin Quest Company.

on the proverbial horse and galloping off in all directions when you prepare and deliver your presentations.

Throughout all stages of creating *Say It Right,* we tried to do things that make the information accessible and interesting to you, the reader. Therefore, we think you will appreciate the following features of the book:

- The chapters are short.
- Each chapter begins with succinct objectives.
- Extensive white space occurs throughout the book.
- Frequent headings help break up a chapter's content.
- Major points are highlighted within the text to reinforce each chapter's content.
- Illustrations and visuals enhance the content and bring life to the printed page.
- Chapter summaries reflect the essence of each chapter.
- Communications-related quotations from dozens of noted people add spice and variety to the content.

A distinctive feature of *Say It Right* is the exercises at the end of each chapter. Whether you are a practicing business executive or a classroom business student, you will improve your oral presentation skills in direct relationship to the energy you put into the exercises. You probably will not be able to complete all of them, so we encourage you to be selective in completing as many as you can from every chapter.

In the information age, the videotape recorder is an invaluable tool in helping you improve your oral presentations. We know of no better teacher than the videotape recorder, and we advocate your mastering its use as a central element of all activities in *Say It Right.*

As you may have deduced, we have written *Say It Right* with two audiences in mind: the practicing business executive and the classroom business student. We have used the techniques in the book in teaching oral presentation skills to audiences varying from one to several hundred—in both the business world and the business classroom. You can be your own teacher in using the book, or you can rely on a seminar director or a classroom instructor to help you use the book.

We acknowledge the encouragement and support of several individuals who helped with this project.

We thank Craig S. Beytien, senior sponsoring editor for Richard D. Irwin, Inc., for his interest in having us capture our teaching techniques in a book. And we thank Jennifer R. McBride, developmental editor for Richard D. Irwin, Inc., for her encouragement and direction throughout the project.

We give a special thanks to Nina Whitehead, supervisor of the Fifth Floor Word Processing Center in the Marriott School of Management at Brigham Young University. We still have difficulty comprehending how many times she read and reviewed every word, sentence, and paragraph in this book.

The visuals of the book came to life through the genius of our illustrator, Clifford F. Dunston; and we especially thank him for his ability to turn our ideas and his into what we think is beautiful artwork.

Above all, we express thanks to family members who supported us. Garth is indebted to his wife, Sheila, for her support. Kaye is grateful for the support of her children, Rolf and Gretchen. And Ted is appreciative of the support from his wife, Mary Louise.

Garth A. Hanson
Kaye T. Hanson
Ted D. Stoddard

Table of Contents

SAY IT RIGHT

Part III
Delivering the Presentation

Chapter 18

Chapter 19

Chapter 20

PART I
Getting Ready

CHAPTER 1

The Relevance of Oral Communication

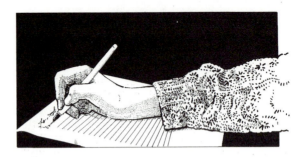

CHAPTER OBJECTIVES

1. To understand the nature of oral communication.
2. To accept the value of having good oral communication skills.
3. To learn about communication phobias as they relate to self-defeating behaviors.

A word fitly spoken is like apples of gold in pictures of silver.

– Proverbs 25:11

With a "whack on the back" at birth, most of us experienced our first attempt at oral communication. Since that time, our various oral communication experiences have fallen somewhere on the continuum of being devastated, experiencing trauma, having a so-so experience, achieving fulfillment, or experiencing exhilaration.

If crying from a "whack on the back" is a form of oral communication, then *oral communication* is an all-encompassing term that potentially includes all the things we do orally to communicate with one another. In addition, oral communication must include the nonverbal things we do to support our oral expressions.

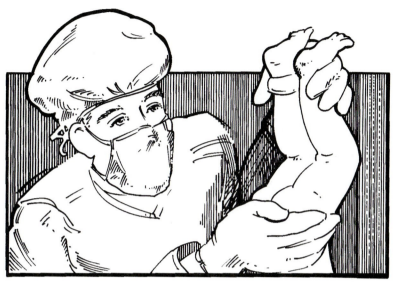

Your first oral communication experience?

Giving speeches, reciting poetry, presenting at business meetings, reading papers at conferences, and teaching college classes are all subsets of oral communication. Obviously, such activities as requesting information about airline flights, ordering a meal in a restaurant, asking directions to the public library, and asking someone for a date are also subsets of oral communication.

Leaders in many fields rank presentation skills as a top need and also lament the quality of the skills they actually find.
– Thomas Leech

> **Oral communication** is an all-encompassing term that includes all the verbal and non-verbal things we do to communicate with one another.

The skills you will learn or improve as a result of studying *Say It Right* are appropriate for all subsets of oral communication. We've written *Say It Right* with two specific publics in mind: students in oral communication classes and practicing business professionals. Naturally, we think the content of the book is appropriate also for any setting in which the reader wants to learn about oral communication.

ACCEPTING THE IMPORTANCE
OF ORAL COMMUNICATION

Many men and women climb their way up the ladder of success by talking their way up it.

Good oral communication skills are important. With that in mind, we naturally hope you will be an interested reader who will absorb everything possible in the pages that follow.

Perhaps you're reading *Say It Right* because you want to. Or perhaps you're reading it because you have to—as a college-classroom student or as a business-seminar participant. Whatever the reason, you may want to keep in mind the following things about good communication skills:

- The ability to communicate effectively is often cited as the single most important criterion for getting promoted in the business world.
- Business workers who have taken a communication course typically rank it as the most valuable of all courses taken.
- Learning to communicate effectively is a life-long learning process.
- Good communicators are made—not born.
- Becoming educated is sometimes viewed as changing one's behaviors. Therefore, improving communication skills comes from changing inappropriate communication behaviors

If you read, practice, and absorb the contents of *Say It Right*, we predict the outcome will be invaluable to you. We make that statement because we know the value of good communication skills and because we've proven the relevance of the techniques you'll read about in the pages that follow.

> **Good communication skills are an invaluable dimension of life. You can improve your communication skills to the extent you can change inappropriate communication behaviors into appropriate ones.**

OVERCOMING COMMUNICATION PHOBIAS

You've probably heard the term *stage fright*. Perhaps you've experienced stage fright when you've been frightened at the prospects of giving a speech or making a presentation.

Stage fright aptly describes the idea of phobias associated with oral communication. A phobia, of course, is an abnormal or illogical fear of something. Following are a few potential oral communication phobias:

- Talking without notes
- Looking the audience in the eyes.
- Forgetting what you want to say.
- Appearing foolish or stupid.
- Being asked questions you can't answer.
- Talking so you cannot be heard.
- Appearing to be shy or hesitant.
- Speaking in a monotone voice.
- Having hecklers in the audience.
- Getting laughed at because of mistakes you make.

The first time I attempted to make a public talk…I was in a state of misery…[M]y tongue clove to the roof of my mouth, and, at first, I could hardly get out a word.

– David Lloyd George, Prime Minister of England from 1916–1922

Communication phobias are dragons waiting to be slain.

If you have any communication phobias, you can take comfort in knowing that you weren't born with them and that you *can* overcome any of them.

All the great speakers
were bad speakers at
first.

– Ralph Waldo
   Emerson

We think our communication phobias are closely related to our self-image and therefore to self-defeating behaviors. That is, if we perceive ourselves as being unable to give a good oral presentation, more than likely we'll give poor presentations.

On the other hand, if we look around us, we'll see individuals just like ourselves who have learned to deal with communication phobias. If these people (our classmates, friends, coworkers, etc.) have learned to deal with any particular phobia, they've changed their behaviors.

To do that, they've convinced themselves of the value or need for change; and they've convinced themselves they can change. In other words, they've turned from self-defeating behaviors to self-fulfilling behaviors. You may need to talk to yourself repeatedly by saying, "Others have overcome this particular phobia; I can overcome it too."

> **Overcoming communication phobias involves a process of changing self-defeating behaviors into self-fulfilling behaviors.**

Some myths of public speaking:

1. *Good speakers are born, not made.*

2. *Good speakers never get nervous.*

3. *Good speakers don't need notes.*

4. *Good speakers don't need to practice.*

5. *Good speakers are actors in disguise.*

6. *I can never be a good speaker.*

Some communication phobias may require considerable practice, but that's part of the skill of developing good oral communication techniques. Developing a skill involves at least the following components:
- Knowledge of desired outcome.
- Guidance in performing the skill properly.
- Initial practice of skill to be learned.
- Appropriate feedback and evaluation of performance.
- Repetitive guidance, practice, and feedback/evaluation.

As you think about any potential communication phobias you might have, you might paraphrase Martin Luther King by saying to yourself, *"I shall overcome."* That's the way to turn self-defeating behaviors into self-fulfilling behaviors.

GETTING THE MOST FROM THIS BOOK

How-to-do-it books for improving oral communication are ubiquitous—they are everywhere. Obviously, we are biased in thinking the book you're reading is one of the best. You'll get the most from *Say It Right* when you study it with the intent of changing your self-defeating behaviors into self-fulfilling behaviors. You'll help yourself do that when you "practice what is preached" in *Say It Right*.

For example, we've found *The FourMat* introduced in Part II to be invaluable in planning and delivering any oral presentation. Whether you're a beginner or a seasoned presenter, we think you'll appreciate The FourMat once you've tried it.

Part III's suggestions for delivering the presentation are quite unique and have proven themselves to be valid countless times in our classes and in consulting situations. We think you'll like the way we've adapted the world of performance to the day-to-day needs of oral communication.

The exercises throughout *Say It Right* are an essential part of changing communication phobias or of changing negative oral communication behaviors. In today's information age, you will profit immeasurably by videotaping yourself as you complete the exercises that have oral outcomes or implications.

*Hearing it,
I forget it.
Seeing it,
I remember it.
Doing it,
I understand it.*

— Chinese proverb

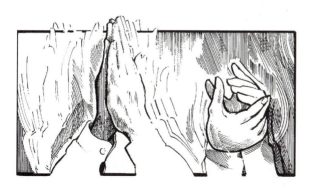

CHAPTER SUMMARY

Good oral communication skills are a must for success in the business world. We are not born with these skills but must learn them. Part of that learning process is to convince ourselves that we can overcome our communication phobias by changing attitudinally from a mentality that fosters self-defeating behaviors to one that fosters *self-fulfilling behaviors*. *Say It Right* contains relevant suggestions and directions to help you achieve success in becoming an effective oral communicator.

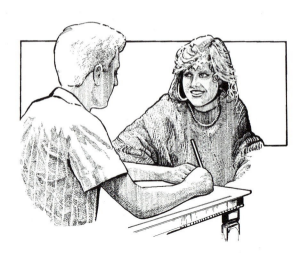

EXERCISES

1. In an impromptu setting, videotape yourself giving a one- to two-minute presentation on one of the following topics:

    If I could live anywhere in the world, I would choose…because…

    The personal trait I most want to develop in the next 12 months is…

    The most important decision I ever made was…

    Community involvement is important because…

    A national lottery should be established because…

    The 55 mph speed limit is necessary because…

    The word *impromptu* implies that you don't plan your presentation. Therefore, the best way to approach this exercise is to pick one of the preceding topics at random or have someone else randomly give you the topic. Allow about two minutes to get your thoughts together before you speak, and then deliver your presentation.

    Try to record yourself on videotape so you can look at the videotape later to see what behaviors you've changed and therefore see the progress you're making as you proceed in *Say It Right*.

2. In an extemporaneous setting, videotape yourself giving a two- or three-minute presentation on one of the following topics:

    • The importance of computer skills in the information age.
    • The value of a line-item veto by the president.
    • The outcomes of community involvement by the average citizen.

- The changes you hope to see in yourself as a result of learning and applying the suggestions in *Say It Right*.
- Effective use of body language.
- Use of visuals and handouts during oral presentations.
- How to change self-defeating behaviors to self-fulfilling behaviors in your oral presentations.

An *extemporaneous* setting permits you to plan your presentation ahead of time. For this exercise, you might want to use note cards or visuals.

Recording yourself on videotape while giving an extemporaneous presentation allows you to look at the videotape later to see what behaviors you've changed and the progress you're making.

3. Interview two or more business executives for their thoughts about the relevance of having good oral communication skills. Use the results of those interviews as the content of an extemporaneous presentation. Videotape this presentation so you can review it as you progress through *Say It Right*.

4. "Think yourself dry" as you make a list of the communication phobias you now have. Describe your current feelings about each phobia. Add to this list as you progress through *Say It Right*. Periodically, review your list and notes and analyze your progress in turning any self-defeating behaviors into self-fulfilling behaviors.

CHAPTER 2

The Realities
of Giving Oral Presentations

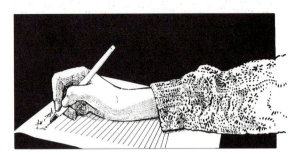

CHAPTER OBJECTIVES

1. Understand the fear factor associated with oral presentations.

2. Recognize the importance of being positive about oral presentation assignments.

3. Prepare to put into practice the techniques for oral presentations contained in *Say It Right*.

Dr. Metzler cleared his throat as he prepared to give his patient, Bill Crowley, a report of the lab tests about Bill's health.

"I have some good news and some bad news," Dr. Metzler said. "Which do you want first?"

"You might as well give me the bad news first."

"Well, the bad news is that you have an inoperable brain tumor; and you have only six months to live."

"That's certainly bad news. What's the good news?"

"You won't have to give any more after-dinner speeches or ulcer-producing presentations to your company's board of directors."

With a sigh of relief, Bill summed up his feelings by saying, "That's the best news I've received this entire year."

Believe it or not, many people state that the fear they have about giving an oral presentation is greater than their fear of death.

Once you have come to grips with the realities of giving an oral presentation, any fears you have about the process will be abated. So what are the realities of giving oral presentations?

GETTING THE ASSIGNMENT

Seasoned presenters sometimes have a lackadaisical attitude when asked to give an oral presentation. In one respect, their attitude might be, "Ho hum. Here comes another one." However, even seasoned presenters face a certain amount of stress at one point or another in the presentation process.

Begin at the beginning and go on til you come to the end; then stop.

– The King, in Lewis Carroll's Alice in Wonderland

Beginning presenters, however, often reflect an attitude of "Why me? What did I do to deserve this misery?"

The process of getting an assignment to give an oral presentation might be likened to the RFP (request for proposal) process used in business and government. Such requests initiate an action that usually results in a written proposal. The proposal then results in additional work on someone's part to fulfill the conditions of the proposal.

In a similar fashion, another RFP is a *request for a presentation.* That request might come to you from a supervisor, from a subordinate, or even from yourself. Rest assured the request will result in an additional workload if *you* end up giving the requested presentation. However, that additional workload is not all bad.

You should view the request for a presentation as a positive, challenging opportunity.

If you consider yourself a beginning presenter, you can take heart by realizing that good presenters are made—not born. Some reality thoughts you might consider when you get a presentation assignment are the following:

You may use different
sorts of sentences and
illustrations before different sorts of audiences,
but don't talk down to
any audience.

– Norman Thomas

- The experience will be beneficial. I'll learn a lot, and I'll take a giant step forward to becoming an excellent presenter.
- Someone must give the presentation. Why not me? I'm flattered I've been asked rather than someone else.
- So what if I don't have an innate speaking ability. This assignment will give me an opportunity to cultivate a talent that can open doors of all kinds for me.
- Am I a pessimist or an optimist? Whatever I am, here's a chance for me to be optimistic by looking at the merits of doing something that will help build my character.

> **Good presenters are made—not born.**
> **The merits of giving oral presentations**
> **far outweigh the negatives.**

OVERCOMING THE INITIAL SHOCK

Beware of the presenter
who is not nervous. A
very important ingredient
to successful presenta-
tion is missing.

Reality will set in soon after you get an assignment to give an oral presentation. In facing that reality, you'll naturally want to do away with the initial nervousness that oral presentations seem to foster. (See Chapter 25, "Stress Reduction," for help with nervousness.)

Nervousness is a natural part of the oral presentation process. Although the process gets easier with practice, some anxiety should always be expected. If you plan to be an excellent presenter, you should adopt the attitude that you must *always* feel some anxiety in the following situations:

1. When you get an oral presentation assignment.
2. While you are preparing your presentation.
3. While you are giving your presentation.

Writers of some language-usage manuals maintain that people cannot be both anxious and eager at the same time. When we think about oral presentations, however, we disagree. Once you are past the shock of being asked to give a presentation, you can legitimately feel both anxious *and* eager.

That is, throughout the process, you should expect to be *anxious*—you should expect to be worried, apprehensive, or uneasy. At the same time, you should be *eager* to cope with the challenge and to revel in the positive feelings of doing a good job. When you have finished giving a good presentation, your feelings will be akin to those of an artist who paints a masterpiece and then stands back to admire it.

Overcoming the initial shock of having to give a presentation should leave you with *residual anxiety.* Such leftover anxiety will be a signal that you *care* about yourself, your listeners, and your message. Those feelings are important and are good; and they are much better than being too lackadaisical, too relaxed, or too far removed from the psychological dimensions of the communication process.

What we're saying, and what you'll read more about in Chapter 25, "Stress Reduction," is that you should not completely get over the initial shock of getting a presentation assignment. You should reach the point of being positive and upbeat about the assignment, but you should also be somewhat "on edge," or anxious, about the assignment.

Speak properly, and in as few words as you can, but always plainly; for the end of speech is not ostentation, but to be understood.

– William Penn

Nervousness is a natural part of the oral presentation process. Good presenters understand the need to be anxious about presentations. They also recognize the desirability of being eager to cope with presentation challenges.

ACCEPTING THE ASSIGNMENT

You should look forward to an oral presentation assignment. Assume a positive attitude and accept the assignment because of the positive outcomes to you and to others. Remember especially that good presenters are noticed and that people who are noticed often get promoted.

The following points are worth considering when you reach the point of accepting an oral presentation assignment:

- Accepting gives you an opportunity to practice your presentation skills—an opportunity for self-improvement.
- Accept graciously and positively, whether you want to accept or not. When you do so, those with whom you work will think much more highly of you than if you accept negatively.

In a sense, every executive speechmaker is an actor, giving a performance for the edification, entertainment, and approval of a highly specialized audience. Since the delivery is as important as the content, an executive needs a bit of the ham.

–Robert E. Levinson

*Mend your speech
a little, lest it may mar
your fortunes.*

– Lear, in
   Shakespeare's
   King Lear

- Giving oral presentations often "goes with the turf." That is, you'll be required to perform if doing so is part of your job. You may as well make the most of your opportunities to improve yourself.
- You're probably justified in being selfish about accepting. That is, when you think about the process, you'll come up with interesting answers to the question of "What can I get out of this assignment?"
- In accepting, you should believe that what you have to say is important. Sometimes, our messages are important to ourselves only, but even that situation justifies accepting most oral presentation requests.
- Giving good oral presentations is a skill. Over time, any skill can be viewed in the following light: Use it or lose it. If you never accept oral presentation assignments, you will never develop that skill.

**In nearly every situation,
the advantages of accepting oral presentation
assignments far outweigh the disadvantages.
Once you make the decision to accept,
do so graciously and positively.**

PREPARING THE PRESENTATION

The best advice we can give you as you begin to prepare your presentation is not to jump on the proverbial horse and gallop off in all directions.

Obviously, you should have a plan for preparing. In reading *Say It Right*, you'll find scores of useful suggestions to help with that plan. In Chapter 4, The FourMat is the foundation for all these suggestions.

In preparing your presentation, you'll be wise to think about the things that turn you on or off as a listener. You can then try to incorporate those things into your preparation. For example, you probably like to listen to presenters who:

- Are upbeat and enthusiastic about their messages.
- Want to share their messages with other people.
- Dress appropriately for the occasion.

- Exude confidence in their role as presenters.
- Make you feel comfortable and express concern for your needs.
- Are well organized and who lead you carefully through their presentations.
- Give life to their presentations through appropriate visuals, interesting "war stories," and effective body language.
- Make you think about their messages and make you want to act in relation to their messages.
- Realize when the time has come to end the presentation.

Brainstorming is clearly a part of preparing presentations, as you'll read in Chapter 6, "The Brainstorming and Grouping Processes." The following directives are often appropriate during the brainstorming process:

- Think yourself dry.
- Read yourself full.
- Then think yourself dry again.

Another dimension of brainstorming is to get help from colleagues—ask for their opinions and input. If colleagues are willing, have them do a "brain dump" by writing down, in thought phrases, all the thoughts they have about your topic.

Obviously, practice is part of preparing your presentation. Perhaps the best practice is when you practice in front of a video camera. In addition, you can practice in front of a mirror; in front of family members, friends, or colleagues; or even in front of pets.

The old adage that "practice makes perfect" is a distinct component of preparing. However, a better adage for you to adopt throughout *Say It Right* is "perfect practice makes perfect." Think about it!

Be sincere; be brief; be seated.

– Franklin D. Roosevelt

Speak clearly, if you speak at all; Carve every word before you let it fall.

– Oliver Wendell Holmes

Say It Right **contains scores of suggestions to help you prepare your presentations. For now, as you think about preparing presentations, keep in mind the things that turn you on as a listener, plan to use brainstorming techniques when you prepare, and make arrangements to use video equipment to help you prepare. Above all, get ready to master The FourMat in Chapter 4.**

GIVING THE PRESENTATION

Say It Right contains scores of suggestions to help you actually give presentations.

As you read further, we recommend you assume you are the author of the suggestions and directives in *Say It Right*. That will help you internalize the suggestions and directives so they become common knowledge to you. From that point, you can then practice what you preach as you implement the suggestions and directives.

Cultivate ease and naturalness. Have all your powers under command. Take possession of yourself, as in this way only can you take possession of your audience.

– Charles Reade

We also recommend you "assume the mantle of an expert presenter." In the eyes of some people, appointed or elected leaders often are covered or enveloped in an aura of leadership expertise. That is, they have assumed the mantle of a leader.

When you assume the mantle of an expert presenter, you will realize that, in spite of any perceived inadequacies on your part, you know more than the members of your audience. That is, you are the expert when you are in front of an audience. Therefore, you should assume the mantle and act like you are in charge. You can then make things happen. Successful presenters know how to do that.

> **Internalize the suggestions and directives in *Say It Right* so they become common knowledge to you. Then, in giving presentations, take charge by assuming the mantle of an expert presenter.**

FOLLOWING UP

What goes on after the presentation may be even more important than the presentation itself.

– Thomas Leech

When you truly face the realities of giving oral presentations, you'll realize the value of following up once a presentation has been given. Among the things to consider doing at that point are the following:

- Write down your reactions—good, bad, or indifferent—to the presentation.
- Write down the reactions of others to the presentation.
- Save your notes and your visuals.

Other things to consider doing as part of following up are the following:

- If appropriate, create and store the information needed to add the presentation to your resume—including the title of the presentation, the name of the event or organization to whom the presentation was given, the city and state, and the date.
- For appropriate situations, keep a paper trail of what you said, to whom you said it, and when you said it, in case you should ever need this information for personal or legal reasons.
- Write a memo or letter of appreciation to the individuals who asked you to give the presentation.

> **You should not consider a presentation to be complete until you have completed appropriate follow-up procedures.**

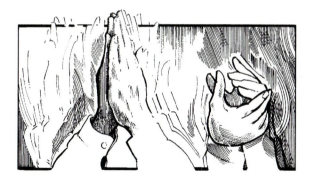

CHAPTER SUMMARY

The realities of giving an oral presentation begin when you get an assignment to give a presentation. You will enjoy the experience much more if you are upbeat about the process and realize good presenters are made—not born.

You should always feel a certain amount of anxiety throughout the oral presentation process. You should expect to be somewhat worried, apprehensive, or uneasy. Those feelings are natural and good. At the same time, you should be eager to accept the challenge and thereby improve yourself and your oral presentation skills.

In the chapters that follow, you'll find scores of suggestions to help you with the presentation process—especially preparing and giving the presentation. Soon, you will be introduced to The FourMat, which will be invaluable to you in coping with the realities of oral presentations.

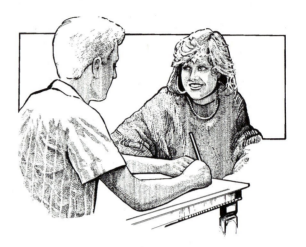

EXERCISES

1. Prepare a short presentation on overcoming the initial shock of having to give an oral presentation. Practice this presentation in front of a large mirror. Critique yourself by identifying anything that might be offensive to a live audience.

2. Prepare a short presentation on the realities of preparing a presentation. Record this presentation on videotape. Identify the things you liked about your presentation in relation to the list of things you probably respond to positively as a listener. (See the list in this chapter under "Preparing the Presentation.")

3. Prepare a short presentation on the realities of overcoming the initial shock of getting an assignment to give a presentation. Give this presentation to a family member, friend, or colleague. Have the listener evaluate your body language, eye contact, and voice quality.

4. Try a brainstorming process to identify the phrases that might be used if you were to give a presentation entitled "The Importance of Being Positive About Oral Presentation Assignments."

5. Organize your thoughts from the brainstorming you did in Exercise 4 and give the presentation while recording it on videotape. Save this videotape so you can critique yourself periodically as you proceed through *Say It Right*.

PART II
Delivering the Presentation

CHAPTER 3 The Start

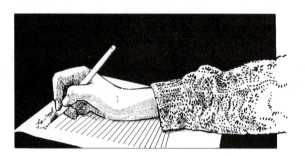

CHAPTER OBJECTIVES

1. Learn what questions to ask when accepting an oral communication assignment.
2. Learn the importance of asking the right questions early in the preparation process.
3. Practice asking appropriate questions to gather all the necessary information the first time.

The phone rings. A voice asks, "Are you busy on the 15th? We need you in Chicago to make a presentation about your project. Can you come?"

You are available and want to make the presentation. How do you make sure you have all the necessary information to do a first-rate professional job?

THE INITIATION OF A PRESENTATION

A presentation begins with the request to "perform." (Every presentation is a performance.) This chapter addresses the step-by-step process of looking at the process of getting started on a presentation.

The best way to get started is to answer six questions. With the answers to these questions, you will have all the information you need to get started on the process of making a winning presentation.

I love being a writer. What I can't stand is the paperwork.

– Peter De Vries

THE FIVE Ws AND ONE H

Who? What? Why? When? Where? How?

News media personnel make a living gathering information from which they often have only one chance to gather *all* the information they need. They initiated an approach called the five Ws and one H as a method of making sure they get all the information the first time. The five Ws and one H, obviously, are abbreviations for the following:

- Who?
- What?
- Why?
- When?
- Where?
- How?

Begin somewhere, you cannot build a reputation on what you intend to do.

– Liz Smith

> **The best way to get all the information you need to get started on your presentation is to ask six questions: Who? What? Why? When? Where? and How?**

Put it before them briefly so they will read it, clearly so they will remember it, and, above all, accurately so they will be guided by its light.

– Joseph Pulitzer

These six questions are designed to gather the information the first time, with some repetition, and to get the presentation off to a good start. This way, presenters will have no surprises associated with missing information as they prepare what they are going to say.

WHO Requested the Presentation and WHO Is the Audience?

Once you have been asked to give a presentation, you need to know who the audience is. Good questions to ask are the following:

- Who are the members of the audience? Are they managers, peers, competitors, etc.? What is their level of sophistication in the subject area?
- Who in the audience is supportive or antagonistic toward me or toward my material?
- Who in the audience is eager or reluctant to hear what I have to say?

Know whom you are speaking to.

> **You need to determine who your audience is— whether the audience is supportive or antagonistic and whether the audience is reluctant or eager to listen.**

WHAT Will the Audience Do with WHAT I Say?

You need to know how listeners will personally process your information. Such knowledge will provide you with the ability to give the information in palatable portions—a process that can mean the difference between success and failure.

Questions that will help you deal with the "what" of getting started are as follows:

- What will the listeners do with the information once they receive it?
- What details or background do they need to have so they can use the information in the most efficient manner?
- What barriers do I need to be aware of to avoid miscommunication?
- What metaphors, visualizations, and other enhancements will work best with this audience?
- What will make this presentation easy for this audience to understand and act upon?

There is no worse lie than a truth misunderstood by those who hear it.

– William James

> **When you determine what the audience will do with what you say, you will be able to give the information in palatable portions— a process that can mean the difference between success and failure.**

WHY Is This Presentation Important for This Group at This Time?

The "why" question in getting started ties closely into other parts of this chapter but needs to be addressed so you can make sure everything is covered. Some of the "why" questions are the following:

- Why is this topic important at this time?
- Why am I the one selected to deliver this topic at this particular time?
- Why have the listeners chosen this presentation to get this information?
- Why are these people present and not others?
- Why are we in this location and not somewhere else?

WHEN Is This Presentation to Be Given?

Timing is especially important to the success of the presentation because the timing affects how the material is used. All the "when"

A powerful agent is the right word. Whenever we come upon one of those intensely right words in a book or newspaper the resulting effect is physical as well as spiritual, and electrically prompt.

– Mark Twain

questions are based on the assumption you are being asked to present because the information is important for some subsequent event, which is almost always the case. Some of the "when" questions to be considered are as follows:

- When will the presentation be given—that is, what is the date, time of day, length of time expected, etc.?
- When is the presentation being given with regard to the sequencing of other related information? What has come before and what comes after your presentation?
- When is the presentation being given in relationship to other functions such as meals, happy hours, and other activities?
- When will the results of my presentation be put into effect?

> **All the "when" questions are based on the assumption you are being asked to present because this information is important for some subsequent event.**

WHERE Will the Presentation Take Place?

By answering the "where" question, you will know where the event will take place in relation to the physical facilities. Knowing this information will permit you to prepare without the need for further worry about these details. Some "where" questions are the following:

- Where will the presentation be made—that is, street address, building number, room number, directions for getting there, and time of arrival including flying, driving, walking, and processing time to get where I need to be?
- Where will I find answers to my equipment needs—that is, how will the availability of such things as electrical outlets, extension cords, sound systems, projection equipment, computer terminals, etc. affect my presentation?
- Where will the audience sit—that is, what kind of audience seating will I have?

Answering the where question in getting started will help ensure that you get to the presentation on time and that you can start on time.

HOW Will This Presentation Be Made for Greatest Effect?

Information can be delivered in a variety of ways. Many factors limit the delivery options. The presenter must make some decisions that will help in selecting the most successful delivery technique.

Give me the right word and the right accent and I will move the world.

– Joseph Conrad

The presenter should select the most successful delivery setting.

Some of the "how" questions to help determine the most successful delivery procedures are as follows:

- How sophisticated is this audience? Do audience members know much of what I know; are they ill-informed on my presentation topic; or are they somewhere in between?
- How open is this audience to a variety of presentation methodologies? Can I be flexible, or do I have to adapt myself to their traditional presentation ways?
- How will this audience interact if I put the listeners in a "U" shape rather than in rows of chairs? Do they need tables, or can they write on their laps?
- How will members of the audience discuss concepts if I present an idea to them so they know I want their input, or had I better stay with a lecture mode?
- How will members of the audience respond to technology as a

Genius begins great works, labor alone finishes them.

  – Joseph Joubert

way of presenting information—such as computer-driven projectors, TV, videotape, etc?

• How will the audience respond to some radicalism on my part, or do I need to stay closely in line with traditional thinking?

CHAPTER SUMMARY

The difference between the almost right word and the right word is really a large matter— 'tis the difference between the lightning–bug and the lightning.

  – Mark Twain

The six major, easy-to-remember questions involving the five Ws and one H are a very effective way of getting all the information the first time, so the presenter can get a good start in preparing the presentation. Presenters often lose a lot of credibility as they stumble through the repeating process of going back to the requester to get information that should have been collected on the first call. Additionally, a solid preparation requires complete information from the beginning.

You will notice the six questions include a certain amount of overlap in the information collected. That happens by design and will assist you in getting all the information you need. You will give a better presentation if you collect too much information rather than too little. Also, the same conclusion reached from different points of view may increase your ability to make a winning presentation.

The questions of Who? What? Why? When? Where? and How? should be committed to memory and asked frequently. They are not difficult to remember, and they will do much to get you started with your presentation.

EXERCISES

1. The next time your instructor or your supervisor gives you a presentation assignment, ask and get answers to Who? What? Why? When? Where? and How? Make notes of your results and compare the results with comments in this chapter.

2. Create a form that will help you ask appropriate questions in accepting presentation assignments. Make the five Ws and one H questions a central feature of the form.

3. Attend a formal presentation and attempt to answer the five Ws and one H questions as though you were the presenter. Observe and analyze instances in which the presenter failed to answer any of the questions adequately.

4. Interview an experienced presenter and ask how problems that are discussed in this chapter are solved. Make notes of your interview and discuss the results of your interview with class-mates or fellow workers.

CHAPTER 4 The FourMat

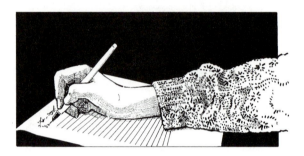

CHAPTER OBJECTIVES

1. Learn the rationale behind The FourMat.
2. Learn the procedures for using The FourMat.
3. Memorize the sequence of The FourMat.

RATIONALE FOR A PRESENTATION FORMAT

The executive who plans the work and then works the plan usually gets good results. As a presenter, you'll get comparable results if you plan your presentation and then follow your plan.

As you probably suspect, the process of putting a good presentation together can be frustrating and time consuming. When you must give a presentation, you'll usually have to sandwich its preparation among the numerous other things you do as part of your job or daily routines. Extra time is seldom available for the preparation process. Therefore, you need to use your preparation time as efficiently as possible—you need a plan to follow so you can save time and frustration.

> ## You may have to spend a lot of time in preparing to give a successful presentation.

As a presenter, some of the things you will have to worry about are the following. They are all directly related to a presentation format.

- Determine the purpose of the presentation.
- Identify the major points to be made.
- Identify the support for each of the major points.
- Develop an outline for the material to be presented.
- Decide upon the recommendations to be made.
- Decide how to begin the presentation.
- Determine how to "tell the listeners what you are going to tell them."
- Decide how to conclude the presentation—how to "tell the listeners what you have told them."

Let us watch well our beginnings, and results will manage themselves.

– Alexander Clark

Set out wisely at first, custom will make every virtue more easy and pleasant to you than any vice can be.

– English Proverb

THE NATURE OF THE FOURMAT

You can prepare presentations quickly and thoroughly by following simple procedures. A helpful approach recommended in *Say It Right* is known as *The FourMat.*

One definition of *format* is "a plan of organization"; and one definition of *mat* is "a border around a picture." The presentation format in *Say It Right* is called The FourMat and is so named because it contains

- Four components that delineate its plan of organization.
- Four borders, known as mats, each of which surrounds, or borders, the four components of The FourMat.

When we build, let us think that we build forever.

– John Ruskin

> ## The FourMat is a time-saving device that will help presenters develop a quality presentation in a short amount of time.

The secret of all power is—save your force. If you want high pressure, you must choke off waste.

– Joseph Farrell

The FourMat contains four sections (mats) consisting of:

- Mat 1—An introduction to begin the presentation.
- Mat 2—The content set to tell the listeners what they are going to be told.
- Mat 3—The body to present the substance or support for the presentation.
- Mat 4—A conclusion to highlight for the listeners what they have been told.

Build The FourMat like a bee builds a honeycomb.

Set all things in their own peculiar place, and know that order is the greatest grace.

– Ralph Waldo Emerson

When used together, the four mats include all the necessary strategy and points that make a successful presentation. Figure 4–1 shows The FourMat in outline form. The FourMat will be briefly outlined below and will be explained in more depth in Chapters 5–16.

Figure 4–1
The FourMat

```
┌─────────────────────────────────────────────────────┐
│                                                       │
│  Mat 1:  Introduction                                 │
│  Setup:                                               │
│  Purpose:                                             │
│  Recommendation:                                      │
│                                                       │
└─────────────────────────────────────────────────────┘
```

```
┌─────────────────────────────────────────────────────┐
│                                                       │
│  Mat 2:  Content Set                                  │
│  Point 1 •                                            │
│  Point 2 •                                            │
│  Point 3 •                                            │
│                                                       │
└─────────────────────────────────────────────────────┘
```

```
┌─────────────────────────────────────────────────────┐
│                                                       │
│  Mat 3:  Body                                         │
│  Point 1 (heading)                                    │
│        A.                                             │
│        B.                                             │
│  Point 2 (heading)                                    │
│        A.                                             │
│        B.                                             │
│  Point 3 (heading)                                    │
│        A.                                             │
│        B.                                             │
│                                                       │
└─────────────────────────────────────────────────────┘
```

```
┌─────────────────────────────────────────────────────┐
│                                                       │
│  Mat 4:  Conclusion                                   │
│  Review purpose:                                      │
│  Review content set:                                  │
│  Review recommendation:                               │
│                                                       │
└─────────────────────────────────────────────────────┘
```

Presenters who memorize The FourMat can fill in the four mats as they transfer thoughts from the mind to paper. Once The FourMat is in place, you can quickly concentrate on the material to be prepared.

In today's information age, time is especially precious. We promise you The FourMat will help you prepare efficiently and give effective presentations.

Drive thy business, or it will drive thee.

– Benjamin Franklin

> # The FourMat simplifies the preparation and the delivery of the presentation.

The FourMat is short, easy to use, and easy to understand. Notice the four major parts of The FourMat.

> Mat 1: Introduction
> Setup:
> Purpose:
> Recommendation:

Mat 1 is the introduction, opening, or beginning. This section introduces the topic to the audience and provides a way for the presenter to begin the presentation.

> Mat 2: Content Set
> Point 1 •
> Point 2 •
> Point 3 •

I can give you a six word formula for success: "Think through things—then follow through."

– Edward Vernon Rickenbacker

Mat 2 is the content set. This section introduces each of the major points in the order of the most important point first to the least important point. Each point is introduced through the use of a heading. In Mat 2, the presenter quickly tells the listeners what will be said.

> Mat 3: Body
> Point 1 (heading)
>   A.
>   B.
> Point 2 (heading)
>   A.
>   B.
> Point 3 (heading)
>   A.
>   B.

Mat 3 is the body of the presentation and represents the major part of the presentation. The major points are discussed in the same order as they are presented in Mat 2. Most of the presentation time is used in this section—up to 80 or 90 percent of the total presentation time. Care must be taken to divide the presentation body into understandable parts.

Mat 4: Conclusion
Review purpose:
Review content set:
Review recommendation:

Mat 4 is the conclusion. In this section, the presenter wraps up the topic, reviews what has been said, and repeats the recommendation given in the introduction. In Mat 4, the presenter tells the listeners what they have been told.

The secret of success is constancy to purpose.

– Benjamin Disraeli

The four mats follow each other naturally during the presentation. The major points are repeated so that in most presentations the listener hears the major points three times. This process is important because listeners cannot go back and reread material as readers do. Repetition is a very important part of successful presentation.

The FourMat organizes the parts of the presentation.

> # The FourMat features built-in repetition because the presenter repeats each major point at least three times.

ADVANTAGES OF USING THE FOURMAT

Don't be "consistent," but be simply true.

– Oliver Wendell Holmes

The FourMat is a proven system to help presenters organize their thoughts as a road map for the presentation. Once you have mastered The FourMat, you'll agree it has the following advantages:

1. The FourMat is a planning and a delivery device that can be used in a variety of presentation situations.

You'll find The FourMat useful whether you're giving a short, informal, five-minute presentation or a long, formal, three-hour presentation. And you'll find The FourMat will organize you whether you're presenting to a committee of a few individuals or to an audience of several hundred listeners.

2. The FourMat is easy to use and easy to understand.

In action be primitive; in foresight, a strategist.

– René Char

The FourMat provides a framework upon which information can be easily placed as it is developed. This framework becomes the presentation outline, which is easily understood by the presenter and the listener.

3. The FourMat produces repeatable presentation successes resulting in satisfied listeners who do not tire of hearing presentations that are planned through The FourMat.

The secret of living is to find a pivot, the pivot of a concept on which you can make your stand.

– Luigi Pirandello

The FourMat is an enabling device that provides the presenter with a way to get concepts delivered quickly, accurately, and completely. Most presenters handle a variety of topics and presentations. Each one needs to sound original. This format allows for that option.

4. The FourMat can be successfully used by presenters from every walk of life.

The procedures of The FourMat are used by professionals from chief executive officers to workers in the smallest office. Successful presenters typically use the procedures reflected in The FourMat. Their goal is to make concise, clear presentations. The FourMat makes that happen.

5. The FourMat offers repetition.

The FourMat repeats important information three times, offers the recommendations at the beginning and again at the end, and provides for efficient use of the presentation time to support each point as it is being made. All these characteristics help the listener understand the purpose of the presentation.

Presentation success is often based on the listener's ability to understand what the presenter has in mind. The FourMat allows the listener easy access to all the information in the presentation.

Be discreet in all things, and so render it unnecessary to be mysterious about any.

– Arthur Wellesley

Listeners expect to be able to understand the presentation by being led through the presentation step by step with the emphasis in the appropriate places. The FourMat achieves that goal.

STEPS IN USING THE FOURMAT

Preparing the presentation occurs in a manner different from the sequence in The FourMat outline. The order of the steps is shown below and will be explained in detail in the following chapters. Preparation efficiency matched with quality of the message is paramount in this preparation order. The steps in completing The FourMat are as follows:

Learn as much by writing as by reading.

– Lord Acton

1. Draw three horizontal lines on a sheet of paper—thereby creating four mats.
2. Write a rough purpose statement in Mat 1.
3. Use brainstorming techniques to list the points you will use to present the material.
4. Limit the brainstorming list to five or fewer by combining or grouping points.
5. Prioritize the points—beginning with the most important and ending with the least important.
6. Write parallel headings for the points and place the headings in descending order in Mat 2.

7. Complete an outline in Mat 3 for the support and visuals for each major point.
8. Write the setup statement and place it in Mat 1.
9. Write the recommendation statements and place them in Mat 1 and in Mat 4, if appropriate.
10. Summarize the concluding statements and place them in Mat 4.
11. Review Mats 1–4 and add any missing details.
12. Practice the presentation.
13. Give a successful presentation.

CHAPTER SUMMARY

Know first, who you are, and then adorn yourself accordingly.

– Epicetus

Most successful presenters use a format for the delivery of presentations. The FourMat shown in this chapter provides a way to organize your thoughts quickly so your audience can easily understand your message.

When you memorize the procedures in The FourMat and use The FourMat often, your presentations will be easy to develop, easy to understand, and successful in getting results.

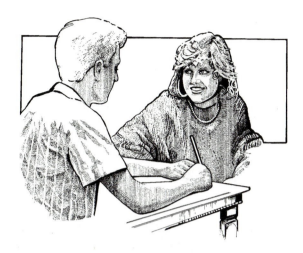

EXERCISES

1. Commit The FourMat to memory.

2. Practice using The FourMat on an imaginary presentation every day for the next three days. Choose ordinary, realistic topics such as the following:
   - The roles of red lights in traffic control.
   - The rationale for buying a dozen bagels.
   - Justification for buying a snow shovel in July.
   - The desirability of sending children to summer youth camps.

3. Listen in a meeting or in a class to questions being asked. As an oral presentation, prepare answers to those questions using The FourMat.

4. Use The FourMat to guide you in answering questions in a meeting or in a class.

5. Using The FourMat, make a presentation based on a paper you have previously written.

6. Using The FourMat, introduce a friend to someone else.

7. While listening to a presentation in real life or from radio or TV, take notes. Then, using The FourMat, prepare a presentation based on your notes.

8. Read an article in a news magazine. Assume you are going to make a presentation of the material in the article. Using The FourMat, prepare a presentation based on the material in the article.

CHAPTER 5 The Purpose Statement

CHAPTER OBJECTIVES

1. Learn what a purpose statement is.
2. Know how and when to use the purpose statement.
3. Know why the purpose statement is important.
4. Read some examples of purpose statements.

Mat 1: Introduction
Setup:
Purpose:
Recommendation:

Mat 2: Content Set
Point 1 •
Point 2 •
Point 3 •

Mat 3: Body
Point 1 (heading)
   A.
   B.
Point 2 (heading)
   A.
   B.
Point 3 (heading)
   A.
   B.

Mat 4: Conclusion
Review purpose:
Review content set:
Review recommendation:

The first information you will put in The FourMat is the purpose statement.

The purpose statement gives the scope of the presentation in one or two sentences. A purpose statement clearly tells listeners what they should expect from the presentation and also tells them what is expected of them. The purpose statement is especially useful in helping the presenter focus the presentation.

Without a purpose statement, you have nothing to say.

A purpose statement clearly tells the audience what you have determined the presentation to be.

*I learn by going where I
have to go.*

– Theodore Roethke

The purpose statement is directly related to the needs of the audience and does the following:

1. Announces the intent of the presentation. In a real sense, the presenter makes an informal contract with the audience via the purpose statement. Through this statement, the audience knows what the presenter will discuss.
2. Provides a short analysis of what the presentation contains.
3. Notifies the audience that the presenter knows what is to be accomplished in the presentation. That is, notice is given that the presenter will fulfill the informal contract made with the audience.
4. Gives direction to the preparation and delivery of the presentation. Every word and point of the presentation should move to fulfill the goal stated in the purpose statement.

> **The purpose statement provides the basis for an informal contract between the presenter and the audience.**

CHARACTERISTICS OF THE PURPOSE STATEMENT

A good purpose statement has the following characteristics:

- Relates directly to the needs of the audience (see Chapter 3, "The Start").
- Occurs early in the introduction of the presentation and is repeated in the conclusion.
- Leaves no doubt about the direction of the presentation.
- Describes the content of the presentation succinctly and accurately in as few words as possible.

*"Mean to" don't pick no
cotton.*

– Anonymous

> **The purpose statement describes the content of the presentation succinctly and accurately.**

WORDING OF THE PURPOSE STATEMENT

The wording of a purpose statement can vary from a direct reference to the word *purpose* to a variety of alternatives. The statement often includes the word *to* plus an action verb to form an infinitive. The presenter's challenge is to simply state the purpose without being offensive or elementary in the delivery. Although the position of the purpose statement may vary in different presentations, it usually follows the setup statement.

To be understood, use a purpose statement.

Persuasive or "bad-news" presentations are examples where the purpose statement may come later in the presentation. In each of these instances, the presenter can plan on some resistance to the presentation plan. Delaying the purpose statement provides the presenter with some time to present a case before the audience can build resistance. These situations occur only about 10 percent of the time.

A = r + p (or Adventure equals risk plus purpose)

– Robert McClure

During the delivery, the purpose statement usually follows the setup statement.

EXAMPLES OF PURPOSE STATEMENTS

Examples of purpose statements are as follows:

Example 1: My purpose today is to describe the process we should use to purchase the Pioneer Street property.

Example 2: We are meeting today to discuss how we plan to buy the property on Pioneer Street.

Example 3: The buying process for obtaining the Pioneer

Street property is quite complex and needs to be discussed in some detail. That is why we are meeting today.

Notice the above purpose statements are quite simple, but are also comprehensive. The purpose statement should interact smoothly with the setup statement and sometimes can be included with the short opening statement—in the same sentence.

An example of a purpose statement in the opening sentence is the following:

> *John asked me to talk to you about the need for a new copy machine and the procedures for training our staff to use it efficiently.*

Consciousness of our powers augments them.

– Marquis de Vauvenargues

The purpose statement can be a part of the opening statement, sometimes even in the same sentence.

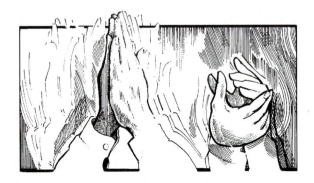

CHAPTER SUMMARY

The trouble with the world is that the stupid are [confident] and the intelligent full of doubt.

– Isaac Bashevis Singer

The purpose statement succinctly tells the audience the purpose of your presentation and directs the preparation of your presentation. During the presentation, the purpose statement usually comes early in Mat 1. In fact, the purpose statement can sometimes be in the same sentence with the opening statement. Usually, the audience needs to know the purpose as early as possible.

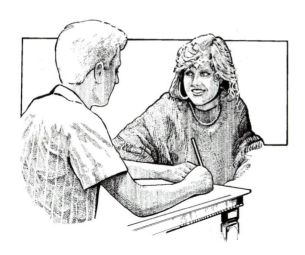

EXERCISES

1. Select a topic for which you will prepare a presentation. Create a purpose statement for the presentation.

2. Listen to a presentation given in your community or in the media. Listen for the purpose statement in that presentation. Write it down. Critique it. Suggest an improved purpose statement if you feel it can be improved, or explain why you think it is good.

3. You have been asked to help someone prepare a presentation. Write a one-page set of instructions to help your friend create an effective purpose statement.

4. Videotape a two-minute presentation giving instructions about how to prepare a purpose statement.

CHAPTER 6

The Brainstorming And Grouping Process

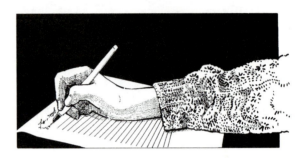

CHAPTER OBJECTIVES

1. To learn what brainstorming is.
2. To learn how to brainstorm major points.
3. To learn what the grouping procedure is.
4. To learn how to perform the grouping procedure.

Mat 1: Introduction
Setup:
Purpose:
Recommendation:

Mat 2: Content Set
Point 1 •
Point 2 •
Point 3 •

Mat 3: Body
Point 1 (heading)
   A.
   B.
Point 2 (heading)
   A.
   B.
Point 3 (heading)
   A.
   B.

Mat 4: Conclusion
Review purpose:
Review content set:
Review recommendation:

?

THE NATURE OF BRAINSTORMING

Brainstorming is the popular name for identifying the points to be covered in a presentation.

According to *Webster's Tenth New Collegiate Dictionary*, brain-storming is "a group problem-solving technique that involves the spontaneous contribution of ideas from all members of the group." We find brainstorming to be a useful tool for individuals as well. In short, brainstorming is a process of listing all the ideas one or more people can come up with concerning a topic.

We promised we could help make the presentation process faster. Brainstorming is one way that occurs. A professor once tested how brainstorming speeds preparation. She had two MBA classes back-to-back. In the first, she assigned a five-page paper on "Why Choose an MBA," which was due the next Wednesday. She asked the students to keep track of how long it took them to write the paper. In the second class, she made the same assignment, except she had the students brainstorm the topic for 10 minutes before they left the classroom.

When the classes returned the next Wednesday morning, she found the first class had taken about 3 hours each to write the assignment. The second class had taken about 1–1/2 hours. The only difference was the brainstorming.

Brainstorming—even a short list—when the assignment is received, cuts down the preparation time needed.

!

The need for brainstorming to identify major points is intense if the presenter is to be successful. The purpose of brainstorming is to identify the major points to be included in Mat 2 of The FourMat.

THE PROCESS OF BRAINSTORMING

Four successful ways of brainstorming are as follows:
- Topic phrases
- Clustering
- The evolutionary process
- Sticky notes

Mistakes are the portals of discovery.

– James Joyce

The Topic-Phrases Process

Write your ideas as short phrases. Work as quickly as possible— paying no attention to the value of the idea or the way it is written. Just write enough to know what you were thinking when you made the note.

If you are working in a group, have someone go to a flip chart, whiteboard, or chalkboard and write as rapidly as possible, while the rest of the group calls out ideas that may be used as points in the presentation.

Brainstorming identifies the possibilities you might consider in supporting major points in a presentation. Left in their collected state, the brainstormed ideas are not very useful. These collected ideas need to be put into related groups that, when organized appropriately, can be used to help the presenter prepare a successful presentation.

Whatever you can do, or dream you can, begin it. Boldness has genius, power and magic in it.

– Johann Wolfgang von Goethe

Clustering

Clustering is a process that often appeals to the right-brained, visually oriented presenter. Let's suppose you need ideas because you are preparing a presentation on the value of oranges from the point of view of a consumer. Begin by drawing a circle and placing the topic or concept within it.

Half of the failures in life arise from pulling in one's horse as he is leaping.

– Julius Have

oranges

Then, draw lines out from the circle with topic words at the end to stimulate ideas. Some good words are the questions journalists use to get to the heart of a story.

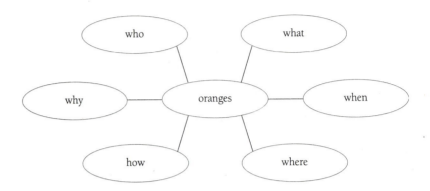

Now, write around the word everything that comes to mind. For example, when you consider the *who* of oranges, you may write *growers, consumers, pickers, workers,* etc. Then, move to the *why* of oranges and write *health, taste,* etc. Continue until your ideas are depleted. Proponents of clustering like the organization that begins to develop and the sense of seeing things all at once.

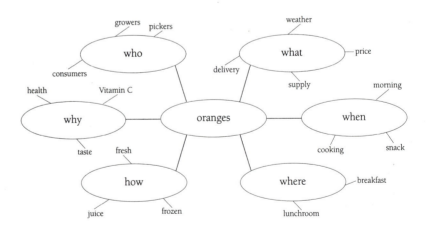

The Evolutionary Process

Try to identify two to five major points you might make concerning your topic. Then, try to identify up to four subpoints for each of the major points. Finally, create as many subpoints as you think you need. In the process, you may find that one or more of the subpoints will become major points.

Through the evolutionary process, you can quickly identify appropriate major points and subpoints for a presentation.

The Sticky–Notes Process

On a sticky note, write a possible major point to support your presentation topic. Then, write a second possible major point on another sticky note. Continue the process until you have as many as 12 major points on 12 sticky notes—and more if necessary.

The value of using sticky notes is that you can quickly arrange and rearrange points as often as you like.

Sticky notes enable you to arrange and rearrange points
efficiently and effectively.

THE GROUPING PROCEDURE

The key to a brilliant presentation is to limit the topic to no more than five most important points.

Most presenters feel very good about their own ideas and have a tendency to like them—*all of them.* Presenters who do a poor job often use all available ideas. Presenters need to learn how to select the points of real importance. Some teaming with a respected colleague to brainstorm and to group the ideas is of great value, especially in the early stages of a presenter's career.

Grouping is a very personal experience. This experience is complicated because an absolutely "just-right" answer seldom exists. Presenters have many options for presenting any topic. Every presenter will have a different style and background that may alter the number and types of points used to support a presentation.

> **Grouping and limiting ideas is not an optional exercise. Presenters simply must do it.**

The grouping of points is a procedure that directly follows brainstorming. Like brainstorming, the grouping procedure can be done alone or in teams. Initial grouping can be easily done in medium- to small-sized groups. Final grouping needs to be done in very small groups or alone.

Grouping is best conceptualized as a "tree" organizational chart. The main point is on top; the subpoints are in the second line; and the sub-subpoints are in the third line. When points are properly grouped, the presenter is able to do a very brief overview by reading the organizational boxes and lines.

> **Grouping is best conceptualized as a "tree" organizational chart with lines and boxes.**

A three-point chart based on the topic of purchasing a copy machine looks like Figure 6–1.

To add depth and length to a presentation, a presenter simply adds the subpoints with their appropriate support. The challenge is

Figure 6-1

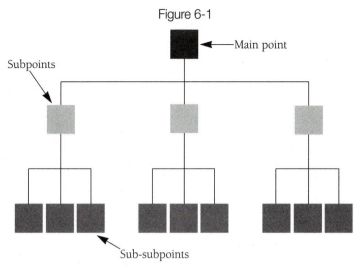

The grouping process resembles a "tree" diagram.

to work with the right amount of support at the right time and place and to take the right amount of time for the presentation. The challenge is met when the presenter makes proper use of the five-or-fewer rule.

Panic can strike the presenter who prepares a presentation of any length and discovers during the meeting or the program that the time will be cut short. If the organization of a presentation is in place, the presenter can easily adapt to the situation.

For example, assume a three-point presentation with support arranged according to Figure 6–2:

Only it seems to me that once in your life before you die you ought to see a country where they don't talk and think in English and don't even want to.

– Thornton Wilder

Figure 6–2

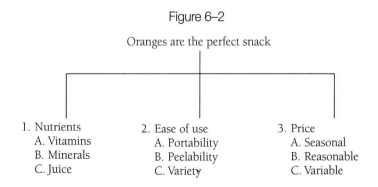

To cope with a shortened presentation time, you have two choices: Cut out one of the points (all of 3, for example) or cut a level of support (all the Cs, for example). The key is having the organization in place and in knowing which points are the most important. Managerial sequence, as discussed in Chapter 9, "Sequence," encourages that the most important points be discussed first. Such sequencing allows adjustment without panic.

> **The challenge is to work with the right amount of support at the right time and place and to take the right amount of time in delivering the presentation.**

There is a time to say something; there is a time to say nothing; but there is no time to say everything.

– Samuel Butler

The following observations will help you group ideas in an efficient manner:

- Keep the number of major points between two and five. Members of an audience have difficulty handling more than about five major points at any one time. The option of presenting more than five major points is generally not acceptable. If you have more than five major points, go through the grouping process until you have five or fewer.
- Adhere to the two-to-five rule throughout the outline of the presentation. A maximum of five major points should be used in any presentation. Also, no more than five subpoints should be used to support any major point; and no more than five sub-subpoints should be used to support a subpoint throughout the presentation.
- Use the two-to-five rule as a simplicity tool. The rule is specifically designed to make the points crystal clear to both the presenter and to the audience.

> **Every major point can be divided into "workable" groups of two to five subpoints.**

The following suggestions will help you group your ideas appropriately:

- Know what you plan to achieve with your presentation. Be very familiar with your purpose statement and with the goals of your presentation. Be sure your purpose statement and goals agree with each other.
- Clarify the brainstormed notes. Review all the brainstormed notes to see that your ideas are clear.
- Physically lay out the brainstormed notes so they are all visible. Flipchart pages may be taped to the wall, chalkboard points should be left in plain sight, and sticky notes should be laid out on a table—so all lists are clear and visible.
- Write a heading for each major point in the brain-stormed list.
- Work with *every* piece of information on the brainstormed list by either crossing it off as irrelevant or placing it under one of the newly created headings. You should discard some things; if you don't, you haven't adequately probed the depths of your mind.
- Count the number of major points created to this point. If you have more than five (and you likely will the first time around), see if you can combine some major points, turn some major points into subpoints, create a new major point that will accommodate other major points as subpoints, or delete one or more major points.
- Work with each piece of information to be sure it is assigned its logical place in the outline.
- Repeat the process of reducing the number of major points, subpoints, and sub-subpoints until you have two to five at each level. Do this process by consolidating or eliminating until the number is two to five at each level. This process may take several iterations if the topic is a complex one. The process gets easier and quicker as you gain expertise in working with groups of two to five.
- Study the major points and determine which is the most important. Place the headings in descending order of importance. Prioritize them. Take care to put them in priority order according to your purposes and goals for the presentation.

Additional information you should know about brainstorming is as follows:

To be in hell is to drift; to be in heaven is to steer.

– George Bernard Shaw

- The more you and the audience know about a major point, the less brainstorming will be needed.
- The less preparation time you have, the less the brainstorming will likely be.
- The less the audience knows about the subject, the more important the information will be.
- The more time you have for preparation, the more time you will spend in brainstorming.

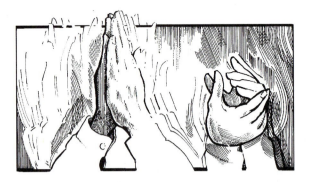

CHAPTER SUMMARY

Every presenter intends to give the best presentation possible with the available resources. Brainstorming and grouping are tools that help create the best possible presentation.

Brainstorming and grouping in the early stages of the presentation's development increase the number of successful presentations. Brainstorming and grouping take time. Good presenters find the time to spend in the development process.

Creating presentations gets easier the more presenters go through the process. Presenters should organize by thinking in groups of five or fewer. The most important points rise to the top.

Natural abilities are the natural plants that need pruning by study.

– Sir Francis Bacon

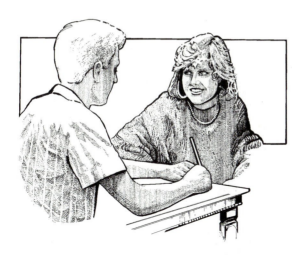

EXERCISES

1. Create a topic about which you could develop a presentation. Brainstorm a list of at least 20 ideas that could be used to develop the topic. Group those 20 points into 2 to 5 points with headings.

2. With the above topic, use all four brainstorming techniques described in the chapter. Compare the four techniques to see which is the most effective for you to use.

3. Select another topic you could make a presentation about. Practice the brainstorming and grouping procedures you have learned in this chapter to identify the points you would use for the development of this presentation.

4. Brainstorm: "All states should have seat belt laws," or "You should bring your convention to _____ (your city) because of the…"

CHAPTER 7

The Content-Set Statement

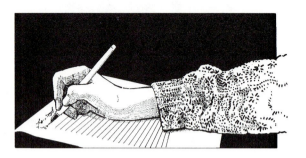

CHAPTER OBJECTIVES

1. To learn what a content-set statement is.
2. To learn why the content-set statement is important to the presentation.
3. To learn how to develop a content-set statement.

Mat 1: Introduction
Setup:
Purpose:
Recommendation:

Mat 2: Content Set
Point 1 •
Point 2 •
Point 3 •

Mat 3: Body
Point 1 (heading)
   A.
   B.
Point 2 (heading)
   A.
   B.
Point 3 (heading)
   A.
   B.

Mat 4: Conclusion
Review purpose:
Review content set:
Review recommendation:

Where do I start?

Mat 1 provides an opening for the presenter and the audience. As soon as both are comfortable with the topic, the presenter moves into a mapping procedure in Mat 2—the content set.

*Words differently
arranged have a differ-
ent meaning, and mean-
ings differently arranged
have a different effect.*

– Blaise Pascal

The content set gives the listeners the major points to be discussed in the presentation. As a part of the introductory statements of the presentation, the content set provides the specific road map of how the presentation will unfold. The content set includes specific steps, usually given in statements of major points to be covered.

**The content set provides the specific road map
of how the presentation will unfold.**

Presentations should be a "no-surprises" activity with listeners working through the unfolding of the presentation together with the presenter.

The content set consists of specific statements that look like headings, all parallel with each other in construction. Each content-set statement describes one section of the presentation. The statements are listed in order of importance, with the most important statement first. The presentation will unfold in the same order the content-set statements are presented.

**The presentation will unfold in the same order
the content-set statements are presented.**

---

*Whenever you see a
successful business,
someone once made a
courageous decision.*

– Peter Drucker

A content-set statement follows the recommendation statement and looks like the following:

Mat 2: Content Set
I have looked into the purchase of a new copy machine for the third-floor preparation room and have found four reasons why we need a new machine. New machines are:
1. Much faster than our current machine.
2. More reliable than what we now have.
3. Equipped with features that are not part of the old machines.
4. Currently being sold at a discount.

RATIONALE FOR THE USE OF CONTENT SET

The content set provides simplification and order to the presentation. The content set also provides transition assistance to the presenter, giving signposts along the way to keep the interest of the audience and to give direction to the presenter.

Clarity is essential when a presenter is making sure the listeners understand. Each member of the audience needs to leave with a full knowledge of the intended message. The content set adds considerably to that clarity.

It is a luxury to be understood.

– Ralph Waldo Emerson

"I will tell you three things about..."

The content set also makes the presentation easy to deliver. A presenter can use each heading as a transitional statement leading from one major point to another. Transition statements can be as follows:

> And now, Point 2,...
>
> or,
>
> Point 2 offers some suggestions as to how we can...
>
> or,
>
> As we move to Point 2, we can see how...

The content set encourages efficient listening and note taking and also provides some help in keeping the speaker on track.

> ## The content set makes the presentation easy to deliver.

THE DEVELOPMENT OF THE CONTENT SET

In the field of observation, chance favors only the prepared minds.

– Louis Pasteur

Chapter 4 introduced you to The FourMat to help you give an effective presentation. In The FourMat, the content set shows headings for each of the major parts of the presentation. These headings can be used as signposts in the delivery of the presentation.

Following are the steps in developing the content set:

1. Know what each of the specific section headings will be.
2. Put each of the headings in a caption format that can be used as a signpost to discuss that part of the presentation.
3. Write all content headings in parallel form.
4. Place all the headings in descending order of importance, with the most important concept first.

There is nothing more dreadful than imagination without taste.

– Johann Wolfgang von Goethe

The Mat 1 introduction and Mat 2 content-set illustrations that follow illustrate the above discussion.

> ## In the content set, place all headings in a caption format.

> Mat 1: Introduction
>
> Setup: Thank you for coming to this executive meeting today. We have been experiencing some problems with the automobile policies for our field marketing staff. The sales staff is currently using personal cars for company business, and we are reimbursing expenses.
>
> Purpose: My purpose today is to discuss the possible need to change our automobile policy to one of owning a company fleet for the marketing staff.
>
> Recommendation: I am personally recommending we go to a company fleet. Our discussion today will either verify that recommendation or suggest we stay with what we have.

Mat 2: Content Set

Content Set: My recommendation is based on four assumptions. They are:

1. The field marketing staff is experiencing a lot of automobile breakdowns.
2. The field marketing staff does not have adequate space.
3. The field marketing staff automobile expenses are too high.
4. Members of the field marketing staff are appearing at clients' doors showing an unacceptable image.

CHAPTER SUMMARY

The content-set statement sets the stage for the material the presenter will cover throughout the presentation. This road map tells the listener, in headline form, the specific points to be covered and the order in which they will unfold.

The content-set statement comprises all of Mat 2 and leads the presenter and the listener into Mat 3, the body of the presentation. Presenters who use The FourMat will find the content-set statement very useful—in preparation as well as in presentation.

In all pointed sentences, some degree of accuracy must be sacrificed to conciseness.

– Dr. Samuel

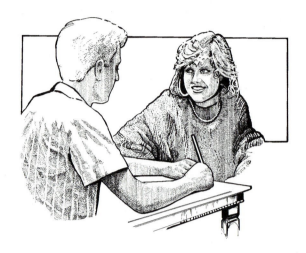

EXERCISES

1. Write a content set for the topic you created in Exercise 1 in Chapter 6.

2. Create three separate forms of setup statements for the above project.

3. Listen to a presenter in your organization or on television. Identify and critique the content set.

4. Write a list of suggestions you might use in creating an effective content set.

The Major Presentation Points

CHAPTER 8

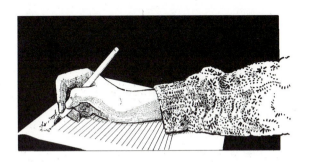

CHAPTER OBJECTIVES

1. To learn what a major presentation point is.
2. To learn how to find the "right" major points for your presentation.
3. To identify four cells of factors necessary to select essential major points.

Mat 1: Introduction
Setup:
Purpose:
Recommendation:

Mat 2: Content Set
Point 1 •
Point 2 •
Point 3 •

```
Mat 3:  Body
Point 1 (heading)
   A.
   B.
Point 2 (heading)
   A.
   B.
Point 3 (heading)
   A.
   B.
```

```
Mat 4:  Conclusion
Review purpose:
Review content set:
Review recommendation:
```

Presentations should generally cover one topic in appropriate depth. Developing a presentation is quite a challenge because simplicity is often more difficult than complexity. That is, *short* is more difficult than *long*. Good presenters are masters of the art of keeping presentations short and centered around one major concept.

> **Developing a presentation is quite a challenge because simplicity is often more difficult than complexity. In other words, short is more difficult than long.**

The value of a principle is the number of things it will explain.

— Ralph Waldo Emerson

Simple presentations can be long or short. Complexity is often caused through proving too many points. The difference between long and short presentations usually involves how many points a presenter uses to "prove" a concept. Depth is determined by how much support is needed to make the point clear.

The FourMat introduced in Chapter 4 has proven successful in thousands of presentations. This format provides a framework for the presentation and makes the concepts clear to organize and deliver. In that format, we introduced space for up to five points of clarification.

This is what I really wanted to say!

This chapter discusses the procedure presenters use to develop their points.

WHAT ARE MAJOR PRESENTATION POINTS?

A presentation point is information a presenter chooses to use to prove parts of the presentation. A good presentation can contain up to five such major points. Very few audiences can handle more than five major points in any one presentation.

Assume you must give a presentation on the need to purchase a new copy machine.

In The FourMat, the introduction and content set of the presentation might appear as follows, including four major points:

To give reason for anything is to breed a doubt of it.

– William Hazlitt

You can discover what your enemy fears most by observing the means he uses to frighten you.

– Eric Hoffer

> **Audiences have difficulties differentiating among points in a presentation if more than five major points are presented.**

Crafty men condemn studies, simple men admire them, and wise men use them.

– Sir Francis Bacon

Mat 1: Introduction

Ladies and Gentlemen. Thank you for coming to discuss the need for improving the output of this department—specifically, the need to upgrade our copy-machine output.

My purpose is to give you some reasons for purchasing new copy machines.

As a result of my investigation into our copy-machine problems, I am recommending we buy new Model Q copy machines to replace the copy machines in the administration buildings.

My first point is…

We hear and apprehend only what we already half know.

– Henry David Thoreau

Mat 2: Content Set

The reasons why we need these new copy machines are:
1. The new copy machines are much faster than our old copiers.
2. New machines are more reliable than our old copiers.
3. New copy machines have added features that are not part of the old machines.
4. New copy machines are currently being sold at discounted prices.

Notice that these content-set statements are very similar to the content-set statements shown in Chapter 7, "The Content-Set Statement." Content set statements *are* major points.

HOW DO I FIND THE RIGHT MAJOR POINTS?

Brainstorming and grouping (see Chapter 6, "The Brainstorming and Grouping Processes") lead to the major points. *Major points are the same as content-set statements* (see Chapter 7, "The Content-Set Statement").

Placed correctly, major points provide the road map your listeners will follow through the strategy of your presentation. You have to know your audience as you search for the right few points for a presentation. When a speaker achieves the goal of using the right few points in a presentation, the listeners will understand each major point.

A thorough study of the presentation topic is essential if the right points are to be found for the presentation. Brainstorming is a good way to begin the search for the appropriate concepts to use in supporting the major points.

As discussed in Chapter 6, "The Brainstorming and Grouping Processes," brainstorming is a popular way for finding new ideas. *Brainstorming* is the popular name for finding a maximum number of the possible major points for a presentation. Finding the appropriate major points is based on the answers to the following questions:

1. How much do you know about the topic you are about to present?
2. How much does the audience know about the topic you will be presenting?
3. How important are the major points in the presentation as a factor of what you expect to accomplish with the presentation?
4. How much time do you have to prepare the presentation?
5. How much time do you have to give the presentation?

Be careful how you interpret the world: it is like that.

– Erich Heller

Facts are facts and will not disappear on account of your likes.

– Jawaharlal Nehru

Fundamental progress has to do with the reinterpretation of basic ideas.

– Alfred North Whitehead

> **Placed correctly, major points provide the road map your listeners will follow through the strategy of your presentation.**

The presenter needs to be able to do the following if the correct major points are to be selected:

1. Identify what the listeners expect to hear in relationship to the topic at hand.
2. Present the major points in a logical manner—logical, that is, from the listener's point of view.
3. Select major points from as large a group of options as possible to assure all the possible points have been considered.
4. Weigh any differences between presenter and audience perceptions so the points are audience oriented.

Life is a great big canvas, throw all the paint you can on it.

– Danny Kaye

> **Present the major points in a logical manner— logical, that is, from the listener's point of view.**

Having precise ideas often leads to a man doing nothing.

– Samuel Butler

The following presenter/audience matrix compares two presenter factors with two audience factors. It is very useful in identifying how much effort you should put into the development process. The presenter/audience matrix is shown in Figure 8–1:

Figure 8–1
Presenter/Audience Matrix

	Audience knows little	Audience knows much
Presenter knows little	1	3
Presenter knows much	2	4

Audience knows little Presenter knows little

Cell 1—This situation could occur when a group is embarking upon a new venture, product, idea, or direction. A presenter could be assigned to "investigate the possibility of," "research the validity of," or "find out about" a specific person, place, or thing.

Preparation is a challenge because the presenter starts without knowing much about the topic. The presenter prepares by speaking with people who know; reading periodicals, journals, and books; or beginning a research project. This type of presentation usually takes the maximum amount of time to prepare, and brainstorming is a critical event.

In Cell 1, the presentation development should involve many outside people and resources in the process. The presenter does not begin as the expert but might end up being the person who knows the most about the subject.

Communication is and should be hell fire and sparks as well as sweetness and light.

– Aman Vivian Rakoff

Preparation in Cell 1 is a challenge because the presenter starts by knowing very little.

Presenter knows much Audience knows little

Cell 2—This situation occurs when the presenter is the expert and the audience wants to know more about a topic. Being an expert presenter provides some ease in content development but is very difficult to keep simple. Most expert presenters assume audiences know more than they actually know, so presenters often speak "over the heads" of the audience. Such "experts" as engineers, doctors, accountants, and lawyers are frequently accused of this behavior.

In this instance, brainstorming is a matter of determining what level of "proof" is needed to provide a clear and precise presentation.

Being an expert presenter provides some ease in content development but is very difficult to keep simple.

Audience knows much Presenter knows little

Cell 3—The wise presenter will leave this situation alone if that option is possible. A common form of Cell 3 occurs in formal settings in which the presenter is being "examined" on what he or she knows.

> **The wise presenter will leave the situation in Cell 3 alone if that option is possible.**

The challenge for the presenter is to determine what the audience wants from the presentation. The brainstorming occurs with people who have been in that situation before and who hopefully know the audience. Once the presenter finds out what is expected, the emphasis of the presentation should be in satisfying the needs of the audience.

The presenter should identify the points the audience is keying on. "I don't know" could be a very wise response in a question-and-answer session. Too many "I don't know" comments can destroy the presenter's credibility, however.

It is terrible to speak well and be wrong.

– Sophocles

> **The emphasis in Cell 3 is to find out what the audience wants and to satisfy the needs of the audience.**

Presenter knows much Audience knows much

Cell 4—In Cell 4, both the presenter and the audience know a lot about the topic. This situation is probably the most challenging of any of the four cells and occurs where both groups are looking to learn more than they already know. The brainstorming process should be extensive, as both the presenter and the audience are looking to expand their horizons.

An example of Cell 4 could occur when the presenter is on the leading edge of a concept. For example, assume everyone is working on a research project to discover how to make a better bicycle frame. Assume further the presenter has found a competitor's product that will cause the presenter's company to lose a lot of money unless a way is discovered to compete with the product.

In a product meeting, the presenter, the supervisors, and the peers identify some questions that need answers. The presenter has been selected to collect the research and make the presentation. Some members of the audience are willing to help collect information and help the presenter prepare the presentation.

He that leaveth nothing to chance will do few things ill, but he will do very few things.

– Halifax

> **Cell 4 is probably the most challenging of any of the four cells and occurs when both groups are looking to learn more than they already know.**

CHAPTER SUMMARY

Major presentation points are information a presenter uses to prove parts of the presentation. Understanding the audience is a key part of selecting the correct points in any presentation.

Knowing the cells in the two-by-two presenter/audience matrix, and knowing the answers to questions about the audience, will provide valuable information for finding the effective major points for your presentation.

Successful presentations begin in the preparation stage where the presenter selects appropriate major points that are strategically placed in the presentation.

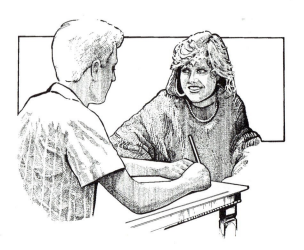

EXERCISES

1. Listen to a presentation and identify the major points the presenter uses. Write an evaluation of how well the major points are used in the presentation.

2. Identify a presentation topic you might present. Examine the audience and situation and place the presentation in one of the cells shown in the presenter/audience matrix. Write some paragraphs about how you identified the proper cell.

3. Write a memo to your supervisor or instructor discussing each of the four cells in the presenter/audience matrix. Add your opinion of how each cell would affect the way you would personally approach a presentation in each situation.

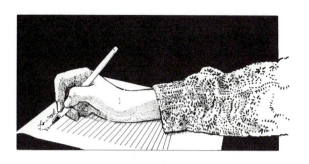

CHAPTER OBJECTIVES

1. Learn what sequencing is.
2. Learn the steps involved in sequencing the points in a presentation.

Mat 1: Introduction
Setup:
Purpose:
Recommendation:

Mat 2: Content Set
Point 1 •
Point 2 •
Point 3 •

Mat 3: Body
Point 1 (heading)
   A.
   B.
Point 2 (heading)
   A.
   B.
Point 3 (heading)
   A.
   B.

Mat 4: Conclusion
Review purpose:
Review content set:
Review recommendation:

Time—A great manager: it arranges things well.

– Pierre Corneille

An important step you will take in giving any presentation is to decide upon the sequence for the presentation information. Determining the sequence will help you give a logical, well-organized presentation.

Read this manual and you'll understand.

You'll develop the sequence through the strategy you create. Knowing the audience and anticipating how the audience will react to the presentation information are all-important when you determine the sequence of the points in the presentation.

SEQUENCE DEFINED

Sequencing, in basic terms, is the process of determining which point comes first and the order of subsequent points in a presentation. All successful presenters select an appropriate sequence in their delivery of the points to give the listeners the information they need in the order they need it.

Two sequence formats are most often used. They are the managerial sequence and the scientific sequence.

First say to yourself what you would be; and then do what you have to do.

– Epicetus

Managerial Sequence

The material in *Say It Right* teaches primarily the managerial sequence, which is aimed at the business professional who wants the important material up front with no surprises as the presentation unfolds.

The FourMat discussed in Chapter 4 achieves the managerial-sequence goal. In using The FourMat, you'll introduce the subject, state the purpose, announce the recommendations to be made, and tell how the presentation will unfold to prove the points being made.

I can teach you how to make lots of money!

Features of the managerial sequence are:
1. Lead with the purpose and the recommendation.
2. Use a strategy that opens every point to the listeners.
3. Make the points in descending order of importance and explain them clearly.

When using The FourMat, presenters give the important material first so the information will be laid out clearly.

Scientific Sequence

Vigorous let us be in attaining our ends, and mild in our method of attainment.

— Motto of Lord Newborough

Another sequence used by some presenters is an indirect, scientific presentational format that leads the audience through the presentation and ends with conclusions and recommendations. Most business presenters find the scientific presentation style less than satisfactory.

Features of the scientific sequence are:
1. Present your material so as to save your conclusions and recommendations until after you have presented your data and procedures.
2. Include all details essential to the scientific logic.
3. Support each point thoroughly with proven information.
4. End with conclusions and recommendations.

Delayed/Bad News Sequence

Presenters sometimes find times when the real purpose of the presentation needs to be delayed until a foundation for the presentation is laid. Such a sequence requires carefully implemented strategy to reveal the purpose at the right moment. Such a sequence is called "delayed/bad news" sequence.

The delayed/bad news sequence is used in high-pressure selling and in delivering bad news. The high-pressure selling, although being used less and less as we approach the 21st century, requires a series of agreeable statements prior to stating the real purpose of the presentation. Examples of high-pressure presentations occur on the doorstep, over the telephone, or in highly implusive buying situations.

The bad-news sequence requires a series of setup statements declaring established situations prior to the delivery of the bad news.

Examples of bad news occur in employment firing situations, denial of significant requests, explaining of serious situations (such as the announcement of a terminal illness from a doctor to a patient), and any presentations that announce less-than-positive situations.

The following are features for the use of delayed/bad news presentations:

- Delay the purpose statement until a substantial base has been established. The audience needs to know where the bad news is coming from.
- Move quickly through the preliminary concepts, usually so the audience has little time to get to the purpose statement before you do.
- State the bad news clearly. Leave no room for doubt.
- Make the presentation as short as is reasonable.
- End on an amiable note, if possible.

THE SEQUENCING STEPS

The sequencing process involves three steps, as follows:

1. Identify the appropriate points to sequence.
2. To support the purpose, lead with the most important point and then progress through the points in order of importance based on value to the audience.
3. Support the most important points more than the less important points.

Do the duty which lieth nearest to thee! Thy second duty will have already become clearer.

– Thomas Carlyle

1. Identify the Appropriate Points to Sequence

Identifying the major points to make in a presentation is discussed in Chapter 8, "The Major Presentation Points." Clearly, knowing what these points are is essential to the sequencing process. Once the points are in place, you can make the appropriate decisions as to how the points are to be laid out.

2. Lead with the Most Important Point

Leading with the most important point is a basic part of the sequencing process. As such, presentations should not be approached as mystery novels in which the listener waits until the end to find out "who did it."

Business listeners are usually very busy and have little time to "figure out" how the presentation is unfolding. They prefer to spend their

Get the facts first. You can distort them later.

– Mark Twain

time being concerned about the points being made. The FourMat logic makes sense to the business audience. Leading with the most important point and then proceeding to the other points in order of importance is the key to that logic.

The most important point must be determined by the perceived values of the audience. Successful presenters make many contacts with members of the audience prior to the presentation, if possible. These contacts will provide information that will help the presenter determine the sequence of the points from the listener's point of view.

> **The FourMat is very popular with business presenters and audiences because it allows presenters to make and to sequence points in a logical and simple manner.**

3. Support the Most Important Points More Than the Less Important Points

In the modern world of business it is useless to be a creative original thinker unless you can also sell what you create. Management cannot be expected to recognize a good idea unless it is presented to them by a good salesman.

– David M. Ogilvy

All points are not equal in the value they have for the audience. If you elect to make four important points where the introduction takes 18 minutes to present, each support item could get 3 minutes, as follows:

Point 1	Support 1 (3 min.)	Support 2 (3 min.)	Support 3 (3 min.)	Total (9 min.)
Point 2	Support 1 (3 min.)	Support 2 (3 min.)		(6 min.)
Point 3	Support 1 (3 min.)			(3 min.)

With this approach, you will spend approximately one-third more presentation time with Point 1 than you will with Point 2. You will spend twice as much presentation time with Point 2 than with Point 3, etc.

If we assume each support item receives three minutes in the presentation, Point 1 with three support items will get nine minutes, Point 2 with two support items will get six minutes, and Point 3 with one support item will get three minutes. (These are approximate times, as few presentations are timed to this exactness.)

Presentations seldom can be successfully placed into a time formula. The times above should be viewed as suggestions only. Use them as guidelines.

> **The most important point should get maximum "air time" with your listeners.**

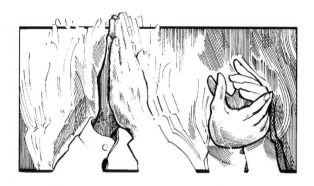

CHAPTER SUMMARY

The sequencing of presentation points is an important part of effective presentations. The procedures described will assist you in being effective in identifying the appropriate sequence for the points in the presentation. Knowing the values of the audience enables you to carefully select the proper sequence.

The more you work through the sequencing process, the easier the process becomes. Simplicity is an important element in making sure the audience knows and acts upon each point. The appropriate sequence of points, simply placed, will lead to successful presentations.

Wait until night before saying it has been a fine day.

– French Proverb

EXERCISES

1. Select a topic for a 10-minute presentation. Select four subtopics to use within those 10 minutes. Arrange them in the sequence of the most important point first and describe why you made these choices.

2. Using a presentation topic selected by your supervisor or instructor, arrange your supporting points in two different ways. Cite possible reasons for changing the sequence in the same presentation.

3. Exchange the sequenced points developed in Exercise 1 with a colleague or fellow student for evaluation. Ask that person to comment on your sequence choices.

4. Select a presentation topic that might be delivered to your colleagues via the managerial sequence.

5. Select a presentation topic that might be delivered to your colleagues via the scientific sequence.

6. Write a one-page memorandum to your supervisor or instructor describing the important differences in Exercises 4 and 5.

Access CHAPTER 10

CHAPTER OBJECTIVES

1. Learn how to define access in a presentation.
2. Learn five access guidelines.

UNDERSTANDING ACCESS

To access something is to emphasize it and thereby make it easy to find and understand. When we apply principles of access to an oral presentation, we emphasize appropriate parts of the presentation. In doing so, we help the listener "get at" the information we're conveying.

In other words, the very act of presenting is an accessing process. Within the presentation process is the need to access—the need to present information so members of the audience can know precisely what points are being made and how they are being supported.

Audiences are becoming more sophisticated as the amount of available information increases. These audiences are demanding a lot of specific information in as short a delivery time as possible. The FourMat provides a way to access your presentation successfully.

You gotta get a gimmick if you wanta get ahead.

– Gypsy

> **Accessed information is information that is easy to get at within a presentation.**

UNDERSTANDING ACCESSING GUIDELINES

Don't take the bull by the horns, take him by the tail; then you can let go when you want to.

— Josh Billings

Being able to access information is one of the most important features of the successful presentation process. Accessing in the business presentation involves five guidelines, as follows:

- Restrict the number of major points in a presentation to two to five.
- Use headings and signposts.
- Use emphatic devices.
- Use white space.
- Use precise, nonexcessive terminology and detail.

Keep up appearances whatever you do.

— Charles Dickens

Access provides the combination for unlocking information.

RESTRICTING THE NUMBER OF MAJOR POINTS

Access is the primary reason we suggest you keep the number of major points low. Typically, a person can efficiently handle a maximum of only five major points at a time. A good presenter will make those points very clear and easy to follow.

Figure 10–1 shows how the concern for simplicity works throughout the presentation—no matter what the length of the presentation. The five-or-fewer rule stays constant throughout the subpoints and sub-subpoints of the presentation.

If you command wisely, you'll be obeyed cheerfully.

– Thomas Fuller

Figure 10–1

Using Two To Five Points In Each Group

I.
   A.
      1.
      2.
   B.
      1.
      2.
      3.
      4.
      5.
   C.
      1.
      2.
      3.
II.
   A.
      1.
      2.
      3.
   B.
      1.
      2.
      3.
      4.
III.
   A.
      1.
      2.
   B.
      1.
      2.
      3.

One of the keys to accessing information in a presentation is keeping each unit to bite-size parts of two to five points, so listeners can group each major point, subpoint, or sub-subpoint in their minds as the presentation progresses.

Keeping the number of subpoints constant under each major point is not the important part. The important part is to keep the number to five or fewer so the listener can remember all of them. In fact, we advise presenters to vary the number so each part doesn't automatically consist of having exactly the same number of supporting subpoints. Some units will have five; others, two or three. Varying the number of supporting subpoints often increases the listener's interest.

By varying the number of subpoints discussed in a presentation, a presenter will keep the audience interested in the format. The process is like varying the number of pictures on the walls of your home.

USING HEADINGS AND SIGNPOSTS IN CLEAR ACCESSING

Don't ever slam the door, you might want to go back.

– Don Herold

Headings in a presentation are designed to separate the points. Headings give the listener a rest from the routine of the body of information. Another term for a heading is a "signpost" that is simply used to provide listeners with a signal that something new or important is happening in the presentation.

Signposts indicate change of thought.

To understand the importance of signposts, imagine you and a friend are going on a theoretical trip from Salt Lake City to Omaha.

If you get in your car and drive, you will eventually get to Omaha. However, think what happens if in Salt Lake you say to your friend, "We're going to Omaha by way of Cheyenne, Scottsbluff, and Lincoln." Already, the trip takes on more meaning for your friend than if you merely say, "We're going to Omaha."

However, an even more meaningful trip will result if you signpost at Cheyenne, Scottsbluff, Lincoln, and Omaha. That is, as you drive along, you say,

- "Here we are at Cheyenne, one of the nicest places in Wyoming."
- "We're now entering Scottsbluff, where I spent the first 10 years of my life."
- "Here's Lincoln. I want you to see the State Capitol Building while we're here."
- "I'm glad to get to Omaha. You'll enjoy seeing where I spent four years during my Air Force career."

As a result of these signposts, the trip has much more meaning than if you merely start in Salt Lake and end in Omaha.

The point is that if we tell listeners where we're going, we'll improve our presentations. And we'll improve the presentations even more if we signpost by signaling,

- "Here we are at Point 1…"
- "Here we are at Point 2…"

A presentation should include a new signpost with every new point, and that should occur very often throughout the presentation. Suggestions for the use of headings and signposts are as follows:

1. Make the headings informative enough to really tell what will be taking place in that section. Instead of *Sales Procedures* as a heading, use a heading like *Procedures for Setting up Sales Strategies*.

> ### A presentation should include a new signpost with every new point.

2. Make headings parallel with each other.

Headings beginning with nouns or verbs are quite common and are easy to make parallel. The popular headings are either noun or verb headings. Here are some examples:

Noun headings:

Procedures for setting…

Methods for developing…

Personnel policies for creating…

Never draw your dirk when a blow will do it.

– Scottish Proverb

If you would be pungent, be brief; for it is with words as with sunbeams—the more they are condensed, the deeper they burn.

– Robert Southey

Verb headings:

    Use a procedures manual for…

    Develop methods for…

    Create personnel policies for…

Headings beginning with nouns or verbs are quite common and are easy to make parallel.

Respect a man, he will do the more.

  – James Howell

3. Make headings easy to recognize.

    Headings must be emphasized if they are going to act like signposts within the presentation. Following are ways to emphasize headings:

- Number the headings.
  My first point is… and then recite the heading. Begin the next heading by saying, *My second point is…* etc.
- Use the numbered headings in the content set of Mat 2 described in Chapter 7, "The Content-Set Statement." "I have four points to make today:"
    1. (These are the subpoints you use to support your major point.)
    2.
    3.
    4.
- Pause before and after using a heading and recite the heading a little louder, more distinctly, and with movement into the audience, where possible and appropriate.
- Use headings as signposts as if your audience were creating an outline of your presentation as you give it.

Pause before and after using a heading.

---

4. Use visuals to emphasize your headings.

    Listeners usually pay attention to your visuals and remember what they say. A list of your headings in the content set and a visual that states each heading as you proceed are excellent ways of using headings.

USING EMPHATIC DEVICES
AS ACCESSING TOOLS

An emphatic device is a mechanical, verbal, or nonverbal way of emphasizing a point. In writing, bolding, capitalizing, spacing, italics, and large print are all emphatic devices. In oral presentations, volume, pauses, visuals, gestures, body language, and movement are emphatic devices.

You must look into people as well as at them.

– Lord Chesterfield

Following are some ways you can use emphatic devices in a presentation:

1. Use a louder-than-normal voice to introduce a point and then move back to your routine voice. (See Chapter 21, "Voice.")
2. Pause at the end of the previous point, state the new point, and then pause briefly prior to beginning the detail of the following point. (See Chapter 29, "The Role of Silence.")
3. Move forward into the audience as you introduce the new point. (See Chapter 20, "Body Language.")
4. Use a visual in introducing the new point, while gesturing toward the visual with emphasis. (See Chapters 12 and 13, "Visual Support" and "Visual Aids Usage.")
5. Use silence where appropriate. (See Chapter 29, "The Role of Silence.")

USING WHITE SPACE
AS AN ACCESSING DEVICE

White space in a presentation is silence, as discussed in detail in Chapter 29, "The Role of Silence." Speakers often have considerable trouble providing enough silence in a presentation. Presenters often think they should fill the air with words because they feel silence is a condition to be dreaded.

Listeners often pay more attention when they are confronted with silence. They look up to see what is going on, wait with some anticipation for the next point, and are ready to proceed with renewed interest.

Think like a wise man, but communicate in the language of the people.

– William Butler Yeats

Following are some suggestions for effectively using white space in a presentation:

1. Vary the speed of the delivery to include some sentences and phrases delivered quickly with other phrases delivered slowly. Some sentences need to be close together while others can have pauses in between. (See Chapter 21, "Voice," for further comments about rate.)

2. Allow time to take notes if the audience is prone to do so. You can announce that time will be available to take notes as you proceed. Then, provide that time as you proceed. Be cautious, however. Your presentation can move very slowly if the pauses are too frequent and too long.

3. Follow your intuition as you watch your audience and allow time for nonverbal interaction with your eye contact. You may ask questions to which you expect no expressed answer but to which the audience needs time to process. Work to see you don't hurry the audience.

Less is more. God is in the details.

– Mies van der Rohe

4. Use silence as white space as you move from one place to another on the "stage" of the presentation. Sometimes, you can wisely move without speaking as you move. At other times, you may give yourself an advantage if you speak as you move, carefully.

> ### Listeners often pay attention when they are confronted with silence.

USING UNDERSTANDABLE LANGUAGE AND DETAIL

You never know till you try how accessible men are; but you must approach each man by the right door.

– Henry Ward Beecher

One of the presenter's goals is to use words that are understood by every member of the audience. A paradox may seem to result when a person spends a lot of time learning a sophisticated language but then must reduce sophistication in the presentation. However, that may be necessary if all listeners are to understand.

Following are some suggestions for using understandable language and detail:

1. Use short sentences, short words, and simple ideas.
    In a business presentation, *He went to the office* is better than

---

> ### Listeners cannot respond to information they do not understand.

He took a circuitous route on his morning drive through town on his way to the office.

2. Use a single word or a short phrase where possible. Some examples are
    Because of rather than *based on the fact that.*
    Near rather than *in the vicinity of.*
    Believes rather than *is of the opinion that.*
    Watched rather than *under surveillance.*

3. Be specific in meaning. Use numbers and comparisons where possible.
    Instead of saying *We make the most markers in the world,* say *We make 250,000 markers every day—25 percent more than any other pen producer in the world.*

It is not enough to do good; one must do it the right way.

– John, Viscount Morley, of Blackburn

Presenters must be aware of the listener's need to access the information being presented and work to make the presentation easy to follow.

CHAPTER SUMMARY

Presenters must be aware of the listener's need to access information. You can improve access in oral presentations by

1. Restricting the number of major points in a presentation to two to five.

2. Using headings and signposts throughout the presentation to call attention to each point.

3. Using emphatic devices throughout the presentation.
4. Using white space throughout the presentation.
5. Using understandable language and detail to make points and subpoints crystal clear.

Those suggestions will greatly assist you in making a solid, clear, successful presentation.

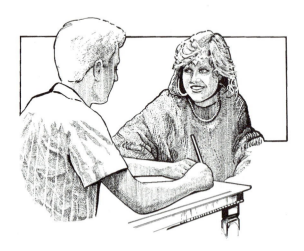

EXERCISES

1. Listen to a presentation and outline the points you hear.
2. Listen to two presenters in a public meeting. Observe how well they access their information and report on your findings in a memo to your supervisor or instructor.
3. Define the following terms in your own words:

   Access

   Wordiness

   Emphatic devices

   Signposts
4. Look at a copy of a popular newspaper or weekly news magazine. Comment on the "access" efforts the editors of that publication have made. Address a two-page memo to your supervisor or instructor on how these techniques might be used in a presentation.

5. Listen to a presenter. List the words or phrases you do not understand.

6. From your everyday conversations, make a list of phrases you hear that could be stated in fewer words.

CHAPTER 11 Support for the Major Points

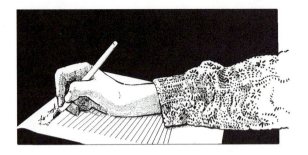

CHAPTER OBJECTIVES

1. To be able to define *support*.
2. To learn how to create support for major points.
3. To learn procedures for simplifying support development.

Mat 1: Introduction
Setup:
Purpose:
Recommendation:

Mat 2: Content Set
Point 1 •
Point 2 •
Point 3 •

Mat 3: Body
Point 1 (heading)
   A.
   B.
Point 2 (heading)
   A.
   B.
Point 3 (heading)
   A.
   B.

Mat 4: Conclusion
Review purpose:
Review content set:
Review recommendation:

THE RATIONALE FOR SUPPORT

After completing the Chapter 6 brainstorming and grouping processes
and the Chapter 7 content-set statements, you are ready to develop
the support for the major points. Support is that part of a presentation
that "proves" each major point.

How can they believe what I say
if I don't use supporting material?

Words are the clothes that thoughts wear— only the clothes.

– Samuel Butler

To understand support, imagine yourself in an audience. Assume the presenter has introduced a topic with the introduction segments and the content set. As soon as the presenter states the content set, your question as a listener is, "Why should I believe those statements?" The support in a presentation provides the answer to that question.

For example, assume a speaker is presenting a topic on the type of vehicle listeners should buy and is specifically "selling" the merits of four-wheel-drive automobiles. Mat 2 provides a content set that includes four points to consider when purchasers buy a four-wheel-drive vehicle:

- Utility
- Roominess
- Expected cost
- Availability

All books are either dreams or swords, You can cut or you can drug with words.

– Amy Lowell

The speaker then begins Mat 3, the body of the presentation, by saying, "Now, Point 1, Utility. A four-wheel-drive vehicle can get you almost anywhere, at any time, in any kind of weather."

The next words the presenter speaks should be an answer to your question, "How is a four-wheel-drive vehicle capable of getting me almost anywhere in any kind of weather?"

One should always aim at being interesting rather than exact.

– Voltaire

Appropriate support, or an answer to your question, might be, "A four-wheel-drive unit is able to provide driving power to each of the four wheels, which maximizes the ability to drive in adverse situations. You can drive this vehicle through snow, mud, mountain terrain, and heavy rain with more confidence than if you were driving a two-wheel-drive unit under the same conditions."

> **The support in a presentation provides the answer to the question, "Why should I believe that statement?"**

In the development of a presentation, the presenter should always ask two questions:

1. How can I prove this point to the listener?
2. How can I be sure the listener understands my points?

If the presenter does well in supporting the presentation, the listener should ask for proof and understanding and then silently say, as he or she listens, "Oh, I see," which could be followed immediately with, "Oh, yes, I agree."

Support materials turn the light on for the presenter and
for the audience.

The support in the presentation is well prepared and presented when each listener responds in this manner.

*Diligence is the mother
of good luck.*

– Benjamin Franklin

> **If the presenter handles support properly, the listener should ask for proof and understanding and then, while listening, say, "Oh, I see," followed by "Oh, yes, I agree."**

DEFINITION OF SUPPORT

Support is information that provides logical proof for the points being made. Support comes from sources such as:

- Statistics
- Examples

- Stories
- Research
- Experience
- Testimonials
- Graphs
- Charts
- Photographs

*Never assume that
habitual silence means
ability in reserve.*

– Geoffrey Madan

Presenters develop understandable support by putting themselves in the shoes of the listener. Simple support is usually the most understandable. Points simply put are most likely to be understood.

Developing simple support should be done so every listener can understand even complex procedures. Simplicity requires:

- Easy-to-understand points
- Clear, simple language
- Defined abbreviations and acronyms
- Accessed information

Simple support is usually the most understandable support.

AN EXAMPLE OF SUPPORT

One experienced speaker was asked to address the topic of time management to a group of eighth graders. The speaker had made time-management presentations before and had volumes of time-managment notes. He had even conducted two-day management seminars on the subject.

This presentation was different because the audience was 30 eighth graders. The time allotment was 40 minutes—in the evening. The meeting was to be held in a school room with lots of chalkboard space. Attendance was optional. In other words, the students were somewhat motivated because they had elected to attend. The students attended with at least one parent.

The key to success in this presentation was to keep the message short and simple. This is the key to success in most presentations. The challenge was to find the time-management concepts that these eighth graders would understand.

> One key to success in most presentations is to keep the message short and simple.

The following questions had to be answered:

1. What time-management challenges does an eighth grader have?
2. Why do these time-management challenges occur in eighth graders?
3. What can eighth graders do to solve these time-management challenges?
4. How can I motivate eighth graders to do something about these time-management challenges?

Once these questions surfaced, the support for the presentation started to take shape.

He who does not know the force of words cannot know men.

– Confucius

SUGGESTIONS FOR SIMPLE SUPPORT

Business presentations are simplified in the same manner. The following directives will help you achieve simplicity in your presentations:

Use Easy-to-Understand Points

The audience expects easy-to-understand information. Presenters often have problems because what is easy for the presenter to understand may not be as easy for the listener.

Highly technical presenters often use a type of shorthand speech containing abbreviations and acronyms, and such presenters make assumptions they think everyone should understand. This shorthand is often not understood by listeners.

In most presentations, abbreviations, acronyms, and assumptions should be spelled out so everyone can understand the points.

Do not accustom yourself to use big words for little matters.

– Samuel Johnson

> Most listeners don't understand abbreviations and acronyms as well as the presenter thinks they understand.

Visuals are usually simpler than words. In the preparation of a presentation, the presenter should be searching for a way to express points visually rather than verbally. The use of visuals is discussed in detail in Chapters 12 and 13, "Visual Support" and "Visual Aids Usage."

Use a Variety of Proof Models

Audiences are more easily convinced when a variety of proof is used— such as charts, graphs, statistics, comparisons, stories, pictures, and videos.

Visuals should usually be used whenever they are clearer than words would be. Presenters need to actively look for ways to use visuals wherever possible. Audiences usually believe what they see before they believe what they hear.

The constant use of long, involved words proves two things: (1) that you're learned, and (2) that you're ignorant of how best to communicate with people.

– Will Comeray

> **Members of an audience will move to action more quickly when motivated by what they see rather than by what they hear.**

Use Clear, Signposted Points

Audiences appreciate knowing where the presenter is going. Signposts assist the audience in following the presentation. Signposts are terms like "My first point is…" or "Let's move to Point 3." These signposts should be separated by the wise use of silence, before and after, as well as by wise increases in voice volume.

The order of the signposts must be logical. Once you announce the order of the signposts in the content set, maintain the same order of the points throughout the presentation. Remember to introduce the most important point first.

Use visuals to emphasize signposts. The introduction of each point provides an opportunity to introduce new visuals. Such a change will increase the effectiveness of signposts.

The difficulty is not to write, but to write what you mean, not to affect your reader, but to affect him…precisely as you wish.

– Robert Louis Stevenson

DEVELOPMENT OF SUPPORT

Time management for eighth graders unfolded as shown in the following boxes.

Mat 1: Introduction

Setup: Thank you for asking me to come and speak to you about time management. I know a lot of young teenagers who would like to be better at managing their time.

Besides having taught eighth graders in the public schools, I have had four eighth graders living with me in my home over the years. I know that one of their greatest problems is to live harmoniously with parents. I am going to begin by asking you what you would give to declare peace with your parents?

Purpose: My purpose this evening is to talk with you about time management, an "adult" term that teaches you how to get your chores done at your house and to get along with your parents.

Mat 2: Content Set

Content set: In the next 40 minutes, we are going to explore some ways to live peaceably with your parents. In doing this, I will assume that you, as eighth graders, can get along with your parents. I'm also going to assume that managing your time is a good way for you to accomplish that.

We will talk about four time-management concepts that will help you get along with your parents:
1. Care about how you use your time.
2. Solve your parents' concerns first.
3. Develop an attitude where you work with your parents, not against them, whenever you can.
4. Enjoy the extra time you will have when you manage your time well.

Body: We will now discuss Point 1—caring about how you use your time.

What gets my interest is the sense that a writer is speaking honestly and fully of what he knows well.

– Wendell Berry

Successful business presentations follow the same procedures. *Simple* and *understandable* are key words. The topic of the presentation is almost always provided by someone else—usually a person with some authority or with a problem to solve. The development of the

Energy and persistence conquer all things.

– Benjamin Franklin

presentation is usually up to the presenter to create and is best addressed through the following procedures. Making the presentation clear and simple is definitely the presenter's responsibility.

- Identify the problems surrounding the topic.
- Identify the specific reasons why the problems exist.
- Identify the specific actions members of the audience can take if they are to solve these problems.
- Identify ways to motivate each member of your audience to perform solutions to the problems.
- Identify a strategy that will most likely bring about the desired results.

Hostile language can kill you as surely as hostile driving can...The problem is that—unlike what happens when you run head-on into a speeding car in the wrong lane—the damage usually takes place slowly, over time, and the wounds aren't readily visible.

– Suzette Haden Elgin

You are now ready to deal with the support for the major points. You have to prove each point with believable and understandable support as you move through the presentation. The development steps are:

1. Evaluate each possible support item and the number of presentation minutes needed to get the message across.
2. Evaluate each possibility in terms of the age and maturity level of the listeners. What will keep their interest and solidify your points?
3. Select the supporting points you will use.
4. Assign a specific number of presentation minutes to each support point.

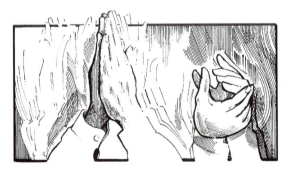

CHAPTER SUMMARY

The guidelines for developing support in a presentation are:

1. Know the audience.
2. Ask the "proof" questions you think the audience will ask as simply as possible.

3. Provide the "proof" as simply as possible.

4. Provide more proof for the earlier points than for the later points.

The appropriate support in the right place at the right time will make the difference between a successful and an unsuccessful presentation.

If a man writes a book, let him set down only what he knows. I have guesses enough of my own.

– Goethe

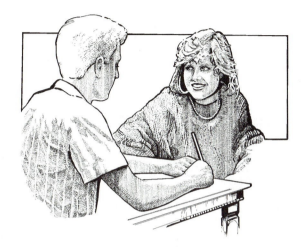

EXERCISES

1. Identify a presentation's major point and create four types of support for the point.

2. Select one support subpoint from the presentation in Exercise 1 and create three different ways to support it using the techniques in the chapter.

3. Listen to a presentation and critique the support the presenter uses.

4. Write five steps you could use for creating support for a presentation.

5. Make a list of 12 abbreviations or acronyms you think every one of your colleagues or classmates will understand. Show this list to 10 or more colleagues or classmates, and ask them to tell you exactly what each item says or means. Write a one-page summary of the results.

CHAPTER 12 Visual Support

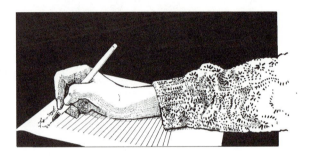

CHAPTER OBJECTIVES

1. Learn the basics of creating visuals.
2. Provide suggestions for illustrations.
3. Develop the appropriate supporting captions.

Visual presentations are much more effective than nonvisual work. Straight copy read at a podium is the least interesting type of presentation. Communication procedures are changing with the times, and some parallels exist between written and oral communication.

A newly recognized axiom in written communication is: "The paragraph is the least effective way to communicate in written communication."

The axiom could also describe the oral presentation without visuals. A presentation without visuals is usually the least effective way to communicate in an oral presentation.

Listeners don't have the option of skipping from visual to visual. They have to listen to what the speaker says. The responsibility to create interest lies with the presenter.

> ## Listeners don't have the option of skipping from visual to visual. They have to listen to what the speaker says. The responsibility for interest lies with the presenter.

An oral presentation without visuals is like a written document that contains words only—no headings, no bulleted items, no enumerated items, and no graphic aids.

Listening to and watching a presentation without visual support is something like listening to a movie on the radio.

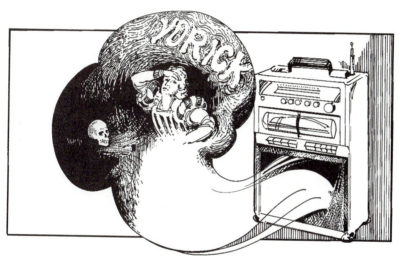

Alas, poor Yorick…I knew him well.

Figure12–1
Do You Want to Read This?

A presentation without visuals is the least effective
and least interesting way to communicate.

There are no facts, only interpretations.

– Friedrich Nietzsche

This chapter describes the role of visuals in an oral presentation. Visuals require appropriate preparation. Good visuals dramatically improve a presentation when they are used appropriately. We encourage the extensive use of good visuals.

> **Use visuals when showing is better than saying.**

THE BASICS OF VISUALS

Let's identify a few basics of good visuals and then describe those basics. We will then show you some visuals and explain how they are created.

Following are a few of the basics of creating good visuals.

"For example," is not proof.

– Jewish Proverb

1. Effective visuals are focused to accomplish specific goals. Each visual should be used with a designated purpose and should be brainstormed for content, purpose, and support using the process discussed in Chapter 6, "The Brainstorming and Grouping Processes." Visuals present a variety of opportunities for clarity and variety, which can make the difference between success and failure in a presentation.

Everything should be made as simple as possible but not one bit simpler.

– Albert Einstein

2. Effective visuals are extremely simple with fewer than six parts. A part is defined as one piece of information—for example, one line of a chart.

Figure 12–2
Effective Visuals Are Focused

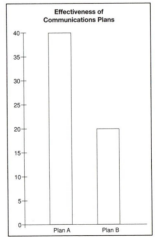

Effective visuals focus on very few points.

3. Effective visuals vary so the data are represented by different types of charts, graphs, and illustrations within the same presentation. Good presenters use a variety of visuals, such as line charts, photographs, and word graphs, within the same presentation.

Hit hard, hit fast, hit often.

– William Frederick "Bull" Halsey

Figure 12–3
Create Simple Charts

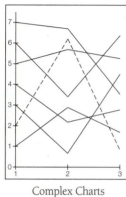 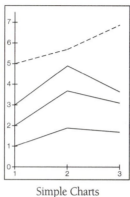

Complex Charts Simple Charts

Line charts are most effective when they are simple. Notice the chart on the left is too complicated, whereas the chart on the right has fewer parts and is more effective.

Figure 12–4
Use a Variety of Visuals

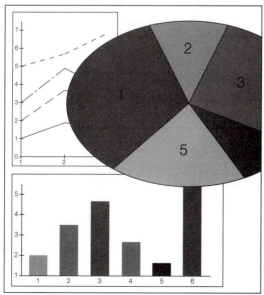

Using several different types of visuals adds variety to your presentation.

4. Effective presentations include a variety of the types of visuals. For example, a presenter can use an overhead transparency, a flip chart/chalkboard presenter-drawn visual, and a video all in the same presentation. Caution: You can use too many types of visuals, which will cause listener confusion. Most presenters err on the side of too few rather than too many.

Too many different types of visuals create visual clutter.

Figure 12–5
Use a Variety of Types of Visuals

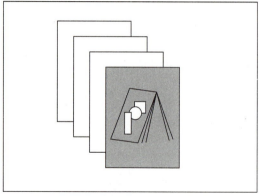

Using more than one type of visual increases the effectiveness of your presentation.

Painting is just another way of keeping a diary.

– Picasso

5. Effective visuals are done in color where possible. Shades of colors are not acceptable when used to separate facts.
6. Effective visuals are easily read in 20 seconds by everyone in the audience—*everyone.*

Limit the color to approximately four basic colors—those with contrast such as black, blue, red, and green.

An unforgivable presenter comment is, "I know that you can't see this but…" Such a comment often accompanies a solid page of unenlarged typewritten copy that has been made into a transparency in a business setting at the last minute. Visuals showing too many concepts also fall into this category.

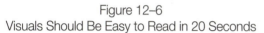

> **An unforgivable presenter comment is, "I know that you can't see this but …"**

Put yourself on view. This brings your talents to light.

– Baltasar Gracian

Figure 12–6
Visuals Should Be Easy to Read in 20 Seconds

Visuals should be simple and readable in 20 seconds.

7. Use the latest technology where you can—but only if you are competent in its use.

Very effective computer-driven visuals that can be operated by the everyday presenter are now in use. These are user friendly and can be driven from a laptop computer, which is easily transportable. Such visuals require projection equipment that is often not easily transportable and may not be readily available.

Figure 12–7
Utilize Technology

Use the latest technology.

CHARTS

Whatever you do kid, always serve it with a little dressing.

– George M. Cohan to Spencer Tracy

The word *chart* is often used as a generic term describing all visual aids—anything that translates words into pictures for better understanding. For our purposes, the word *chart* means a graphic illustration of facts and figures in visual form. A few types of charts are discussed on the following pages.

Bar Charts

A bar chart compares two or more pieces of information through vertical or horizontal bars. Effective bar charts show no more than five or six bars on a single chart. Color or contrasting bars are effective in bar charts.

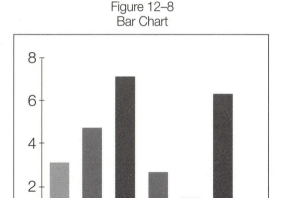

Figure 12–8
Bar Chart

Bar charts are effective in comparing two or more pieces of information.

Pie Charts

A pie chart compares three or more pieces of information where the total of all the information equals 100 percent. The circle is divided into percentages of the 100 percent whole. Effective circle charts show no more than five or six pieces of information. Color or contrasting segments are also effective in the use of pie charts. Colors must be contrasting to show an obvious separation.

If you want to get across an idea, wrap it up in a person.

– Ralph Bunche

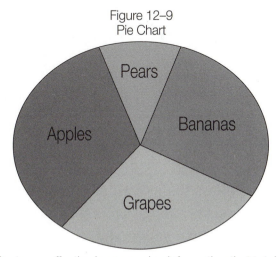

Figure 12–9
Pie Chart

Pie charts are effective in comparing information that totals 100.

Line Charts

A line chart compares several pieces of data shown on a grid. The vertical grid is the "y" axis; the horizontal grid is the "x" axis. As in most charts, simplicity is an essential key to being able to understand a line chart. Color is nice—but not quite as effective as when used in other kinds of charts.

Figure 12–10
Line Chart

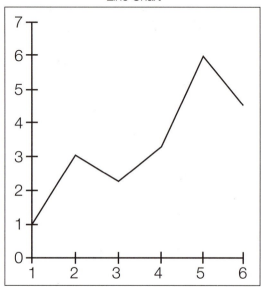

Simplicity is the key to successful line charts.

Organizational Charts

An organizational chart gives a visual description of a management organization. An organizational chart uses lines and boxes to show who reports to whom within an organization.

> ## Charts allow the presentation of a large number of facts and figures in a small amount of time and space.

Figure 12–11
Organization Chart

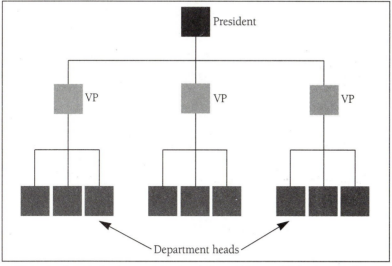

Organizational charts provide visual descriptions of the organization.

ILLUSTRATIONS

Illustrations describe concepts, often in the operation of something, that are difficult to describe in a text. Such illustrations are often produced by professional graphic artists. However, many computer programs are available to allow businesspeople to create their own illustrations. Typical computer-generated illustrations are those that show the flow of liquid through a system or electricity through a circuit.

Set all things in their own peculiar place, and know that order is the greatest grace.

– John Dryden

Figure 12–12
Water Purification Process

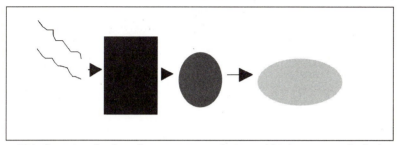

This figure easily describes a process that would take a great deal of time to describe in text.

> **Technical descriptions, complicated networks, and detailed systems can be too complex to describe. With the use of a visual, complex descriptions are presented in a simple and accurate way.**

Following are several suggestions for the use of illustrations.
1. Keep illustrations very simple—the fewer concepts per illustration, the better.

> **Many presenters limit each illustration to no more than six lines of print and no more than six words per line.**

Self-command is the main elegance.

– Ralph Waldo Emerson

2. Use color to demonstrate how certain concepts work: Blue shows blood going to the heart. Red shows blood coming from the heart.
3. Double–check each illustration for accuracy. An illustration is often described by one who is not working with the system on a regular basis. Make sure the illustration you use accurately describes the process you are working with.
4. Label all parts accurately and succinctly. Every function has its purpose and is labeled to describe that purpose.
5. Place all letters, numbers, and labels horizontally so they can be read without forcing the listener to turn the document to read the illustration.

PHOTOGRAPHS

Photographs convey reality. They show what really exists and permit audiences to relate closely to what is being said. Photographs can be developed, miniaturized, enlarged, and placed on overhead projection devices with excellent accuracy and quality.

Following are some suggestions for using photographs:

> **Photographs provide a powerful medium that helps the audience identify with and relate to the information being presented.**

1. Keep the content of the photograph simple. Use each photograph to convey a single point. Keep the background plain and simple.
2. Make the photograph large enough to be seen clearly and easily by everyone in the audience.
3. Use color, where appropriate.
4. Keep photographs focused, sharp, and clear.
5. Use reference points in photographs so the audience can tell how large or small the real object is.

TITLES

All visuals should be shown with titles. Even though a presenter usually introduces a visual by citing a title, every member of the audience should be able to reread the visual with a comprehensive title as the visual is being shown.

Titles should be informative enough to be specific. Single-word titles usually are too general and therefore hinder the clarity of the visual.

Following are examples of appropriate titles:

Not: Introduction
But: "Develop a fleet of company-owned cars"
Not: Costs
But: "Finance the fleet acquisition"
Not: Summary
But: "Advantages of company-owned fleet"

Emotion: ah! let us never be one of those who treat lightly one of the words that most deserve reverence.

– Charles Du Bos

SUPPORTING CAPTIONS

Every visual should have a "persuasive tag" attached to it, usually under the visual. This tag is called a caption. The caption describes what the visual is and does. A supporting caption describes the benefit of the concept the visual shows. The supporting caption does an additional job of selling the concept for the presenter.

> **Supporting captions assist the visual in being able to stand alone; they help the reader understand the visual without reading additional text.**

Figure 12–13
The Supporting Caption

A supporting caption further explains the visual.

COMPUTERS AND VISUALS

An exciting innovation in the visual arena is the use of computers as an integral part of presentations. Presenters often operate a computer in front of the audience with the computer screen showing on a large screen for every member of the audience to see. Data are shown in color while the presenter makes changes to the data in whatever way is needed. This technology, used properly, can greatly enhance a presentation.

Additional presentation skills are required for computer-assisted presentations. These skills include:

- Knowledge of existing computer presentation software.
- Skill in computer operation.

- Preparation skill to include updating data.
- Presentation skills to include appropriate use of the computer during the presentation.

Most of these skills are obtained in seminars, in courses, and on the job. This skill development never ends, as the hardware and the software change so frequently. A discussion of available software is impossible in this text for the same reason. You are encouraged to contact local software and hardware representatives and firms for that information. See Chapter 13, "Visual Aids Usage," for tips on using computers as a part of presentations.

Be prepared.

– Boy Scout Motto

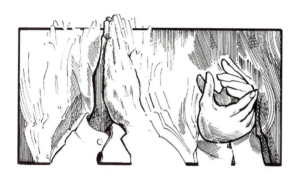

CHAPTER SUMMARY

Visuals are extremely important to the success of most presentations. In this day of visual communication, audiences are used to looking at visual messages. They usually respond positively to presentations that are based on visual images.

Some basics to creating effective visuals are provided in this chapter. Visuals that are focused to the needs of the audience are simple to understand. For variety purposes, they vary throughout the presentation. They are preferably done with color, and they are presented with the latest technology.

Many types of visuals can be used—ranging from a simple bar chart to a more complex illustration. The presenter chooses the visual that will support the presentation in the best way.

Each visual needs to convey its entire message. Descriptive captions make that possible.

Successful presenters work very hard to have the right visual in the right place at the right time. They also incorporate the latest technology in their work and find that the computer is a very useful visual tool in many presentations.

Throw your heart over the fence and the rest will follow.

– Norman Vincent Peale

Visuals add an element of interest and professionalism when used properly. Successful presenters use them wisely.

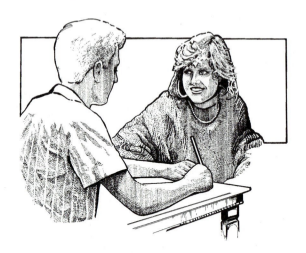

EXERCISES

1. Create an illustration for a five-minute presentation with appropriate headings and supporting captions.

2. Create a photograph for a presentation to someone in your organization showing some condition that needs to be corrected. Use an appropriate heading and supporting captions.

3. Create three headings for the introduction section of a report you have recently written.

4. Create two appropriate visuals for the following information:

    We have sold the following merchandise in the past six months:

    345 model B distractors

    283 model R developers

    103 model Q retractors

    27 model H deliverers

    5 model I enhancers

5. Create a presentation about how to develop appropriate visuals. Assume the presentation will be given to a group of potential speakers.

Visual Aids Usage

CHAPTER 13

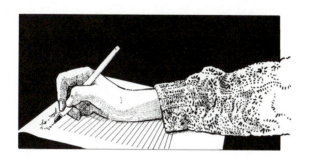

CHAPTER OBJECTIVES

1. Identify eight different kinds of visual aids.
2. Discover advantages and disadvantages to each kind of visual aid.
3. Learn specific tips for visual aid usage.

We live in a visual world. Television has brought the visual world to our living rooms for many years. Newspapers, magazines, and advertising have all sensitized us to the power of the visual message. This chapter is about *how* to use the visual methods at our disposal for presentations.

Another tool for getting attention again and again is the use of visual aids. This chapter is about managing the visuals after they are prepared. We will look at several different types of visuals, discuss the benefits and drawbacks of using each one, and give some tips for easy use. The visuals we will consider are:

- Overhead projection
- Computers and LCD plates
- Flipcharts

- Chalkboards and whiteboards
- Videotapes
- 35 mm slide projection and movies
- Objects and models
- Mounted posters and pictures

OVERHEAD PROJECTION

There are two kinds of light—the glow that illuminates and the glare that obscures.

– James Thurber

Probably the most commonly used visual aid in the United States is the overhead projector. Boardrooms, classrooms, and offices all typically have overhead projectors in them.

I know you can't read this, but...

A new presenter may think the presence of so many overhead projectors indicates the overhead projector is the best possible visual aid to use. That may not be true. Choice of visual aid should be driven by the best possible way to communicate the purpose to the audience.

Don't be guilty of choosing overhead projection just because you think that is what everyone uses.

Advantages:

- Projectors are readily available.
- Transparencies are inexpensive and easy to prepare.
- Transparencies can be written on and changed in front of an audience.
- Color is readily available.
- They are easy to use.

Disadvantages:

- The projector or the presenter can block a listener's view of the screen.
- Bulbs can burn out.
- The fan is sometimes irritatingly noisy.
- Transparencies can be sterile and lack variety.
- Poorly prepared transparencies often are accompanied by the worst possible thing a presenter can say, "I know you can't see this, but…"
- Screens are often not easily seen.

Tips for easy use:

- Test your transparencies on the machine for focus and visibility before your audience arrives.
- After putting a transparency on the projector, move back to the screen to indicate where you want the audience to look. That way you can keep your face toward the audience and you can move out of the way.
- When you're through with a transparency (and won't use another for a minute or so), turn off the machine. Doing that returns the focus to you. *You* are your best visual aid.

What we anticipate seldom occurs; what we least expect generally happens.

– Benjamin Disraeli

COMPUTER PROJECTION AND LIQUID CRYSTAL DISPLAY PLATES

Advances in technology are difficult to keep up with. By the time we learn to use equipment or software, it is often obsolete. However, the up-to-date presenter will be aware of ever-increasing usage of computers to animate and clarify visually. Many programs allow color and movement.

A computer screen in a small boardroom is big enough to be seen. However, in a larger room, you may have to plug into a projection system or use a liquid crystal display (LCD) plate to project onto a screen. Though LCD plate quality is improving all the time, the projection can be difficult to see in some parts of a room, or the colors can fade so the presenters lose more than they gain.

Chance favors the pre-pared mind.

– Louis Pasteur

Advantages:
• Color and animation.
• Control of timing and organization.
• Credibility with current pizzazz.
• Preparation.
Disadvantages:
• You have to know the hardware and software and their capabilities.
• You must have lead time to prepare.
• Things can go wrong with equipment.
Tips for easy use:
• Have Plan B in place in case something goes wrong.
• Practice with the program several times.
• Simplify the technical parts of the presentation.
• Scout out the room and the electrical plugs beforehand to increase ease of set up.

FLIPCHARTS

Don't try to fine-tune somebody else's view.

– George Bush

Flipcharts are commonly found in organizations where training and problem solving are common. Flipcharts are an inexpensive way to capture information that can then be taped around walls until the current meeting or project is finished.

Advantages:
• They are inexpensive.

Flipcharts offer unique advantages in some circumstances.

- They are easy to prepare.
- You can create as you go.
- You can use color to increase interest.
- You can create in advance.

Disadvantages:
- Tripod legs get in the way.
- Paper shows wear easily.
- The visuals are not always reusable.
- The visuals are difficult to see in medium- to large-sized rooms.

Tips for easy use:
- Turn up one corner ahead of time for easy movement to the next page.
- Write on every other sheet (or every third sheet) to minimize "bleeding" between pages.
- Stand to the side of the flipchart to gesture or write.
- Write notes in tiny light pencil at the top of the sheet to help you create the visual as you present.

CHALKBOARDS AND WHITEBOARDS

Training rooms, board rooms, and classrooms are usually equipped with either a chalkboard or a white board. As visual aids, they are probably the type we are most familiar with—dating back to our days in the schoolroom. In spite of their familiarity in our lives, presenters have difficulty using them to advantage.

Charm is more than beauty.

– Yiddish Proverb

Chalkboards or whiteboards are available in most conference settings.

Advantages:
- They are available almost everywhere.
- They are very inexpensive to use.
- The writing can be created or changed rather quickly.
- Color is easy to achieve on the whiteboard and is available for the chalkboard.

Disadvantages:
- Chalk dust clings to clothes.
- The presenter has to face the board to write and can be difficult to hear.
- Poor handwriting may be difficult to read.
- The presenter may have to erase to write other material.

Tips for easy use:
- Write only key words.
- Prepare ahead of time, if possible.
- Write in large and legible text.
- Stand to the side and keep turning face toward the audience.

VIDEOTAPES AND CAMCORDERS

The best mirror is an old friend.

– George Herbert

Videotapes and camcorders are increasingly available. As a teaching tool, the videotape is extremely useful.

All audience members are generally valid critics. They know when they see and hear a good presentation. They just don't know what they do themselves as presenters. Videotaping makes that possible—by providing a way for people to get outside themselves and look objectively at behavior. Though most presenters are appalled with what they see themselves do poorly, they also happily discover they do some things amazingly well.

Videotapes that are professionally prepared are also increasingly available. They are useful for teaching processes and concepts and for visually demonstrating support in almost any area the presenter needs.

Advantages:
- Represents a clear, interesting medium.
- Can be prepared by amateurs.
- Presenters can see themselves.
- Information on most subjects is probably available.
- The tapes can be reused.

Disadvantages:
- Videotape equipment is expensive.
- They need special equipment.
- Equipment sometimes malfunctions.
- The screen on the TV is often too small for very many participants to see adequately.

Tips for easy use:
- Be familiar with equipment.
- Set up ahead of time.
- Cue tape to just the short portion you want to use.
- Connect what the listeners have seen to what you are saying.

Few things are harder to put up with than the annoyance of a good example.

– Mark Twain

35 MM SLIDE PROJECTION AND MOVIES

For quality, the use of 35 mm slides or 16 mm movies is still superior. However, most movies are transferred to videotapes these days. (When did you last see a reel-to-reel projector in use?)

Advantages:
- Quality is excellent.
- Durability is excellent.
- They can be reused without loss of quality.

Disadvantages:
- They take lead time to prepare.
- The room must be darkened for use.
- Appropriate equipment must be available.

Tips for easy use:
- Number slides in order on the slide frame. If the slides fall out, you can easily put them in order.
- Know where the room's light switch is.
- Connect what is seen with what you're saying.

No gain is so certain as that which proceeds from the economical use of what you already have.

– Latin Proverb

OBJECTS AND MODELS

Looking at the real thing, or a version of it, is always interesting to an audience. The good presenter can effectively support a presentation by use of objects or models.

Looking at the real thing is always interesting to an audience.

Advantages:
- Clarity
- Hands-on experience

Disadvantages:
- Passing around may disrupt listening.
- Many things are just too small or too large.

Tips for easy use:
- Hold the object up near your face.
- Hold it still.
- Move deliberately through the features on the model you want to show.

MOUNTED POSTERS AND PICTURES

Personally, I am always ready to learn, although I do not always like being taught.

– Winston Churchill

The simplicity of a well-prepared poster is still an interesting visual for an effective presentation. Words, charts, and pictures are effectively used this way.

Advantages:
- Posters and pictures are inexpensive.
- They can be prepared on a computer for a professional look.
- They are typically reusable.

Disadvantages:
- They are usually only effective in small rooms.
- Some lead time is necessary for mounting.
- They are often difficult to transport.

Tips for easy use:
- Have a tripod for the floor or the table.
- Have a plain poster to cover the first sheet.
- Work to the side of the posters.

HANDOUTS

Handouts help an audience study information they see in your presentation. They may be distributed before, during, or after the presentation is completed. The material in the handout may be an outline of the presentation, simple copies of the overhead transparencies, or supplementary material to be read later.

Listeners like to get handouts.

Advantages:
- Listeners can reconstruct what they heard.
- Notetaking is facilitated.

- Listeners have something to carry away to help them remember.

Disadvantages:

- The audience may read instead of listen.
- Passing papers and turning pages can be distracting to the presenter and the audience.

Tips for easy use:

- Manage the use of handouts. Urge listeners to follow along with you, tell them you'll hand material out later, and lead them page by page—anything that helps them know what you want from them relating to the handouts.
- Prepare and distribute the handouts a day or so before the meeting if you want the audience to come prepared.
- Use handouts only if they will help clarify. Don't use them just to have something. In this day of environmental consciousness, wasting paper is wasting trees.

Copy nature and you infringe on the work of our Lord. Interpret nature and you are an artist.

– Jacques Lipchitz

CHAPTER SUMMARY

The demands of living in a visual world require presenters to use visual aids to increase attention and interest. Because no ultimate visual aid is the best for all situations, looking at advantages and disadvantages of various visual aids increases the presenter's abilities to choose the appropriate *visual* for this audience and purpose. Tips for using each type of visual increase credibility and effectiveness.

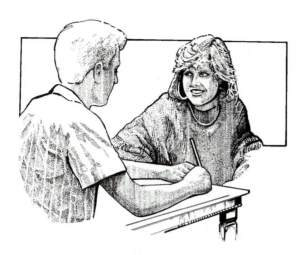

EXERCISES

1. Prepare a five-minute presentation using two different types of visual aids. Give the presentation.

2. Prepare, practice, and present a one-minute presentation using a type of visual you've never used before.

3. Prepare a visual aid you can prepare before the presentation—like overhead transparencies, a flipchart, or 35 mm slides. Practice and present the presentation using the visual aid for notes.

4. Use a visual aid you develop as your presentation unfolds—like a chalkboard or whiteboard, a flipchart, a videotape, or an object or model. Plan how you will use the visual and give the presentation.

5. Collect three handouts from presentations you attend. Evaluate how these handouts were used, and write suggestions for improvement.

CHAPTER 14   The Setup Statement

CHAPTER OBJECTIVES

1. Learn how to develop a setup statement.
2. Consider some long and short setup statements.

Mat 1: Introduction
Setup:
Purpose:
Recommendation:

Mat 2: Content Set
Point 1 •
Point 2 •
Point 3 •

Mat 3: Body
Point 1 (heading)
    A.
    B.
Point 2 (heading)
    A.
    B.
Point 3 (heading)
    A.
    B.

Mat 4: Conclusion
Review purpose:
Review content set:
Review recommendation:

With the meat of the presentation in place, you are ready to polish Mat 1, the introduction, and Mat 4, the conclusion.

Each step of the presentation should be carefully planned to produce the presentation results you are seeking. What is the audience expected to do as a result of the presentation? The more specific the expectation, the better.

> ## At the outset of the presentation, the presenter should know what action is expected of the listener.

THE PRINCIPLES OF A SETUP STATEMENT

Members of a business audience usually make a major decision within 30 seconds of the time the presenter begins the presentation. The listener's decision usually is, *"I am or I am not* going to listen to this

Forewarned, forearmed.

– Benjamin Franklin

presentation. The presenter's job is to do everything possible to make sure the listener *will* listen.

The first task is to get the listener's attention. Because most members of business audiences have come to your presentation thinking of a host of other things, your opening statement needs to get everyone thinking about one concept—your presentation.

Because you already know a lot about your audience (as discussed in Chapter 3, "The Start"), you know how the audience feels about your topic. Those feelings dictate how you will begin. You should keep the setup statement part of your presentation as short as possible.

> **Because most members of business audiences have come to your meeting thinking of a host of other things, your setup statement must get everyone thinking about one concept— your presentation.**

An incomplete setup statement: "Honey, do we have enough gas?"

THE FUNCTIONS OF A SETUP STATEMENT

The two major functions of a setup statement are:

1. To provide the listeners with an immediate reason for attending the presentation.
2. To provide the presenter with a transition tool to get from the beginning of the presentation into the rest of the presentation.

Reasons for Attendance

Listeners come to presentations with several questions about why they should be in attendance. The setup statement should answer their questions, giving them the incentive to stay and listen. The following are questions the setup statement should answer:

- Why am I here?
- Why is this presentation important to me?
- Does this presentation have anything directly related to what I am doing?
- Will I change anything I do in the future because I am listening to this presentation?
- What is expected of me because I am listening to this presentation?

For all your days prepare, And meet them all alike, When you are the anvil, bear—and when you are the hammer strike.

– Edwin Markham

An appropriate setup statement: "Honey, do we have enough gas in the car?"

By anticipating these questions and answering them in the setup statement, you will give your listeners incentive to pay attention to the rest of the presentation.

The reasons a listener is in attendance are not always obvious. The specific reason may be masked in a broader reason.

For example, a meeting may be called to discuss an efficiency problem in the sales division. As the presenter, you may recommend the purchase of a company-owned fleet of cars that will decrease the number of client meetings the sales staff misses because of personal-car breakdowns. Your setup statement may then be something like the following:

> *"We are here today to discuss how to improve the efficiency of the employees in our sales division. John has asked me to focus on some of the problems we are having in missing important client meetings, especially due to car breakdowns."*

This setup statement clearly identifies the purpose of the meeting and introduces the speaker's role in the purpose of that meeting.

Transition Tool

Reason is also choice.
  – John Milton

The setup statement also provides the speaker with a transition tool into the purpose of the presentation. Presenters need a way to get into the body of the presentation, and the setup statement does that job.

Notice in the above example that a speaker can easily begin the presentation with the words shown. The manager in charge of the meeting could introduce Jim by saying:

> *"We have asked Jim Blakemore (he could be you) to address some of the problems we are having in the sales division. Jim, the next 15 minutes are yours."*

Listeners typically want to be involved in the subject matter of a presentation. They need help with that process throughout all stages of the presentation—but especially at the point a presenter begins.

The first words Jim says constitute the setup statement and go like this:

> *"Thank you John. We are here today to discuss how to improve the efficiency of the employees in our sales division. John (the manager in charge of the meeting) has asked me to focus on some of the problems we are having in missing client appointments, especially due to car breakdowns. The purpose of my presentation this morning is to…"*

This setup statement clearly defines the reason for the presentation and provides a transition tool into the purpose statement.

THE LENGTH OF A SETUP STATEMENT

A setup's length depends on the audience and the amount of time available for the presentation. If the audience knows a lot about what the speaker is saying, the setup statement could be just seconds long. If the audience does not know much about what is going on, the setup statement could be longer.

As a general rule, shorter is better than longer for setup statements. In fact, the entire introduction, including the setup statement, the purpose statement, the recommendation statement, and the content set, should take only up to 10 percent of the total presentation time.

Keep the setup statement as short as possible.

Following are two examples of a setup statement that could be used in the company-owned fleet of cars presentation.

A Long Setup Statement Example

The long setup statement is used when the audience doesn't know much about the problem or the solution. Figure 14–1 is an example of a long setup statement.

Use long setup statements when the audience knows very little about the topic.

The mind's direction is more important than its content.

– Joseph Joubert

What we call results are beginnings.

– Ralph Waldo Emerson

Imagination is more important than knowledge.

– Albert Einstein

Figure 14–1
A Long Setup Statement

Mat 1: Introduction

Ladies and Gentlemen: We are always looking for ways to improve the performance of our sales team. We checked into how our sales representatives get to and from their clients' places of business, as we noted from Martin Johnson's recent activity reports. I quote Martin:

"I have been working with the Horizon Corporation on a possible high-volume sale. I set an appointment with them last Wednesday to finalize the deal. On my way to the appointment, I lost a fan belt off my car and was stranded on the freeway for two hours. (I have been meaning to get the belt replaced but just haven't done it.)

"When I finally called Joe at Horizon, I found they were sorry I missed the meeting. They decided to go with our competition since a decision had to be made at that meeting. We lost a $500,000 deal."

This experience at Martin's expense prompted us to look through all our sales representatives' activity files for the past six months. We found nine additional examples where reps have had problems getting to client appointments on time because of car failure problems that could have been eliminated with routine car maintenance.

Our sales reps are driving their own cars and are trying to save expense money through inadequate maintenance of their vehicles. Perhaps the time has come to move toward the purchase of a company-owned fleet of cars where we can keep the sales people in newer cars and dictate proper maintenance.

The purpose of this meeting today is to…

A Short Setup Statement Example

The short setup statement can be used when the audience knows a lot about the topic. Figure 14–2 is an example of a short setup statement:

Figure 14–2
A Short Setup Statement

Mat 1: Introduction
Ladies and Gentlemen: We have all heard about the recent loss
of a $500,000 sale by Martin Johnson because of a broken $15
fan belt on his car. This is the tenth car-maintenance event
affecting major sales in the last six months. I think it is time to
consider a company-owned fleet of cars for our sales reps.

The purpose of this meeting is to…

**Use short setup statements when the audience
knows a lot about the topic.**

CHAPTER SUMMARY

The setup statement is the initial segment of the presentation and has
two functions. The first is to give the listener a reason to listen. The
second is to provide the presenter with a transition tool.

The setup statement should accomplish its functions in as little
time as possible—shorter is better than longer. Longer setups,
however, are used effectively when the audience knows little about the
topic. The setup statement must set the stage for the presentation.

*I am part of all that I
have met.*

– Alfred, Lord
Tennyson

EXERCISES

In nature there are neither rewards nor punishments—there are consequences.

– Robert G. Ingersoll

1. Listen to a presenter live or in the media. Analyze the setup process. List some suggestions that would improve the setup using suggestions in this chapter.

2. Identify a topic for a five-minute presentation. Create a setup statement for that presentation.

3. Listen to a news broadcast. Identify the setup statements from two news items discussed on that broadcast.

4. Attend a community meeting. Listen to a minimum of two presentations. Write a memo to your supervisor or instructor commenting on the setup techniques for the presentations.

The Recommendation Statement

CHAPTER 15

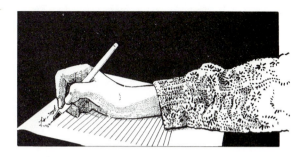

CHAPTER OBJECTIVES

1. To learn what a recommendation statement is.
2. To learn the rationale for the up-front recommendation statement.
3. To learn how to make specific recommendation statements.

Mat 1: Introduction
Setup:
Purpose:
Recommendation:

Mat 2: Content Set
Point 1 •
Point 2 •
Point 3 •

Mat 3: Body
Point 1 (heading)
    A.
    B.
Point 2 (heading)
    A.
    B.
Point 3 (heading)
    A.
    B.

Mat 4: Conclusion
Review purpose:
Review content set:
Review recommendation:

The introduction of a presentation includes three parts:

1. The setup statement.
2. The purpose statement.
3. A recommendation statement that is optional based on the type of presentation you are making.

Choose a road.

A recommendation statement is highly desirable, even though it is optional.

NATURE OF A RECOMMENDATION STATEMENT

A recommendation is a statement of the action the presenter expects from some or all of the audience as a result of the presentation and varies in where it is placed in the presentation.

A clash of doctrines is not a disaster—it is an opportunity.

– Alfred North Whitehead

Each presenter assumes the role of an expert for at least a few moments in front of a given audience. As an expert, the presenter is assumed to have studied the topic at hand and is often expected to make a recommendation as to what to do as a result of having dealt with the subject.

> **You are expected to assume the role of an expert about your topic. As an expert, you should be able to make an educated recommendation.**

Presenters are often expected to introduce the recommendation in the introductory part of the presentation. The purpose of the presentation may be to make recommendations about how to solve specific challenges.

Opinions have vested interests just as men have.

– Samuel Butler

RATIONALE FOR THE UP-FRONT RECOMMENDATION

Business listeners expect to know what action you hope to get from your presentation. Their attention spans are usually short, they expect a lot of information in a short time, and they want to listen only to what they need to hear.

Power is not revealed by striking hard or often, but by striking true.

– Honore De Balzac

By placing the recommendation up front, you will put the audience and yourself on notice that what is discussed will meet the qualifications for making and supporting the recommendation.

*Lessons are not given,
they are taken.*

– Cesare Pavese

The placement of recommendation statements is usually based on two types of sequences for a presentation—the managerial sequence and the scientific sequence (see Chapter 9, "Sequence"). The manager and the scientist differ from each other in several ways. The most obvious difference for the presenter to consider is the way managers and scientists prefer to be given information.

Managers are usually in a hurry and want to know where they are going from the beginning. Their thoughts are, "What are you recommending and why?"

Scientists are concerned about the process. Their thoughts are, "Why are you studying this problem; how did you go about the process; what proof do you have that things are the way you think they are; and, finally, what are you recommending as a result of your work?"

As you study your listeners, you need to determine the sequence they expect in your presentation—a managerial sequence or a scientific sequence. The managerial audience and the scientific audience are typically frustrated with each other's presentation style. The manager wonders what takes the scientist so long to get to the recommendations. The scientist wonders how the business presenter can be so shallow as to give the recommendations up front and thereby mar the process.

Say It Right primarily promotes the managerial sequence for presentations. Business listeners expect to know what action the presenter hopes to get as a result of the presentation. Remember, the scientific sequence is useful for communicating bad news (see Chapter 9, "Sequence").

In addition, business listeners usually have short attention spans in a presentation setting. They expect a lot of information in a very short time. They also want to listen to only what they need to hear to solve the pending problem.

Business listeners expect to know as soon as possible what action you hope to get from your presentation.

Choose this option!

THE SPECIFICITY OF RECOMMENDATIONS

You might naturally ask how specific a recommendation should be. The answer is—as specific as possible! If you intend to purchase the property on Elm Street and if members of your audience need to have that information, you should tell them up front you have made a decision to recommend the property be purchased.

The purpose of your presentation might then be to disseminate the reasons and the procedures for purchasing that property.

Announcing the recommendation to purchase the property will save presentation time. That announcement will also put the audience at ease as you proceed.

The more specific the recommendations are, the tighter the presentation will be. An example showing how a recommendation statement might appear when preceded by a setup statement and a purpose statement is shown below.

Nothing requires a rarer intellectual heroism than willingness to see one's equation written out.

– George Santayana

> **Recommendations should be
> as specific as possible.**

Figure 15–1
Putting the Introduction Together: An Example of the Setup,
Purpose Statement, and Recommendation Statement

Mat 1: Introduction
Ladies and gentlemen, thank you for coming to this executive meeting today. We have been experiencing some real problems with the automobile policies for the field marketing staff. They are currently using their own automobiles for company use with reimbursement going back to them every week.

Our purpose today is to discuss the pros and cons of moving to a company-owned fleet of cars for the marketing staff.

As a result of my study into this matter, I recommend we change our automobile policy. I recommend we buy a fleet of cars for our marketing people in the field. This policy should be implemented no later than six months from now.

So now we'll look at three reasons why we need a company-owned fleet of cars.

CHAPTER SUMMARY

The recommendation statement tells the audience what action the presenter expects as a result of the presentation. The recommendation usually is made in the introduction section but can be given later in bad news instances. The recommendation statement puts both the presenter and the audience on notice that the presentation will provide support for the recommendation.

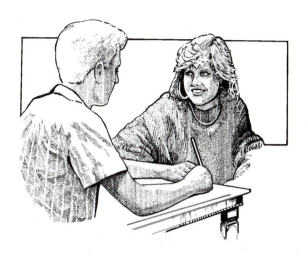

EXERCISES

1. Listen to a presentation and evaluate the extent to which the presenter follows the recommendation suggestions discussed in this chapter.

2. Select a five-minute topic you may present. Prepare an introduction section for that presentation complete with a setup statement, a purpose statement, and a recommendation statement.

3. Practice introductions with a colleague on three topics suggested by your supervisor or by your instructor.

4. Prepare a two-minute presentation giving instructions for making a recommendation statement.

CHAPTER 16 The Conclusion

CHAPTER OBJECTIVES

1. Learn the parts of a successful presentation conclusion.
2. Learn the power of repetition.
3. Learn how to implement each part of a successful presentation conclusion.

Mat 1: Introduction
Setup:
Purpose:
Recommendation:

Mat 2: Content Set
Point 1 •
Point 2 •
Point 3 •

Mat 3: Body
Point 1 (heading)
　　A.
　　B.
Point 2 (heading)
　　A.
　　B.
Point 3 (heading)
　　A.
　　B.

Mat 4: Conclusion
Review purpose:
Review content set:
Review recommendation:

What's this wall doing here now that I've finished my presentation?

The conclusion of a presentation is often a weak part of presentations in American culture. However, the conclusion should be a forceful part of all good presentations. It plays a role with the audience and a role with the presenter.

I do not care how much a man talks if he only says it in a few words.

– Josh Billings

The audience role allows listeners to finish listening. The speaker role allows the presenter to finish speaking. The roles are equally important, but the presenter must direct both roles.

The conclusion section of a presentation allows the speaker to finish speaking and the audience to finish listening. Both parts are important.

REPETITION

Do not, for one repulse, forego the purpose that you resolved to effect.

   – Antonio, in
     Shakespeare's
     The Tempest

No one means all he says, and yet few say all they mean. For words are slippery and thought is vicious.

   – Henry Brooks
     Adams

Successful presenters have learned that repeating presentation points at least three times is a valid presentation technique. These focused points are memorable when clearly stated and repeated.

The greatest challenge for repeating concepts is in the mind of the presenter—not in the minds of the listeners. Presenters typically get bored with the repetition long before listeners. Listeners usually appreciate the presenter's reminder of the important points.

Therefore, the conclusion section of the presentation is packed with repetition. Almost everything in the conclusion has been stated before. Repetition provides the presentational power to drive important points home in the minds of the audience.

Repetition is very important for clear understanding to occur in the mind of the listener.

THE CONCLUSION SECTION

You are encouraged to complete your presentations through a series of four steps. Each step should be quite brief and to the point. Your voice should express a finality to each step so the listener prepares to finish listening.

Following are the four steps in the conclusion section:

1. Repeat the major purpose of the presentation.

Complete the final point in the body of the presentation. Then, briefly pause and begin closing comments by leading with a comment like one of the following:

> *"In summary, my major purpose today has been to…"*

or

> *"In bringing my presentation to a close, I will restate my major purpose. My purpose has been to…"*

or

> *"My purpose tonight has been to…"*

The total conclusion section should be brief, taking no more than 10 percent of the total time allowed for the entire presentation.

---

2. Repeat the headings of the points.

Following the restatement of the purpose, a brief review of the points needs to be made. Using The FourMat, the presenter could repeat the headings for each of the points in one of the following ways:

Mat 4: Conclusion

I will conclude my presentation with this brief summary. My major purpose today has been to…I have explained this purpose by discussing three (or however many points have been discussed) points. These points have been first,…; second,…; and third,…I have discussed them in the order of their importance.

---

or

Mat 4: Conclusion

In bringing my presentation to a close, I will restate my major purpose. My purpose has been to…In support of my purpose, I have discussed three major points. They are (1)…; (2)…; and (3)…

I leave this rule for others when I'm dead, Be always sure you're right—then go ahead.

– Davy Crockett

The greatest truths are the simplest, and so are the greatest men.

– J.C. and A.W. Hare

or

Mat 4: Conclusion
My purpose today has been to…I have supported my purpose by
discussing three points, and I have shown examples in all three
points. The points are (1)…; (2)…; and (3)…

---

*All things flow, nothing
abides.*

– Heraclitus

3. Repeat the recommendation(s) in detail.

The next step is to repeat the recommendation(s). You have probably given the recommendation(s) in the opening part of the presentation. You should now clearly and concisely repeat the recommenda-
tion(s) to drive them home. The recommendation statement might be
as follows:

*"I am recommending we buy the X machine to be delivered no
later than March 1 and to be installed by March 10. To complete
this recommendation, I suggest the following:*

a. *That we finance the X machine using the lease/purchase/buy-
back plan.*

b. *That we plan a three-year pay-out plan.*

c. *That we purchase the maintenance 'B' program.*

d. *That we put John Jones of our Production Department in
charge of the transition period as we bring this X machine
on line."*

*The secret of boring
people lies in telling
them everything.*

– Voltaire

Notice that the recommendation is very complete. All questions
have been anticipated, and the audience knows completely what you
have in mind as you implement your action. This recommendation
may be more complete than the initial recommendation, as you have
built your case during the presentation.

**The recommendation is very complete. You
have made your case; all questions have been
answered; and the audience knows what action
you expect as a result of your presentation.**

A conclusion shows the way.

4. Make a closing statement to allow your listeners to finish listening and to allow you to finish speaking.
A closing statement has two purposes, as follows:
>   a. To tell your audience you are finished with your presenta-
>   tion so they can quit listening.
>   b. To get you gracefully off the stage.

This part of the presentation is quite simple to carry out. Presenters who forget to perform this task leave audiences with an empty
feeling wondering just what to do next. A closing statement follows
the recommendation restatement and goes as follows:

> *"Thank you for your interest in the X machine. I think you can
> see why we need to act right away, and I'm ready to get started."*

or

> *"You can now see why the X machine is so important to our firm.
> We need to act right away to continue our work without interrup-
> tion. I look forward to seeing the purchase order."*

or

> *"This concludes my presentation. We have been worried about
> how to make improvements in the Production Department for a
> long time. This purchase of the X machine will do everything we
> need to do to solve our problems. Your quick action will do much
> to keep our company profitable. Thank you."*

*I learn by going where
I have to go.*

– Theodore Roethke

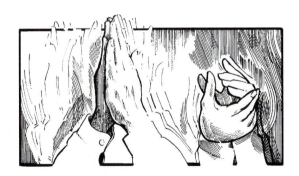

CHAPTER SUMMARY

Every man's work is a portrait of himself.

– Harry S. Truman

Each presenter should make concluding comments to draw the presentation to a close. The FourMat uses four primary parts in the conclusion. They are:

1. Summarize the major points.
2. Restate the purpose.
3. Complete and restate the recommendation.
4. Close the presentation.

The successful presenter realizes the closing of the presentation allows the audience to quit listening and the presenter to quit speaking. Both outcomes are very important to the effective presentation.

EXERCISES

1. Attend a presentation and note how the presenter concludes her or his remarks. Write a one-page report evaluating this closing process.

2. Prepare a two-minute presentation discussing the importance of the closing part of a presentation.

3. Prepare a set of notes from which you could instruct a classmate in how best to close a business presentation.

4. Describe the best presentation close you have ever heard.

5. Describe the worst presentation close you have ever heard.

CHAPTER 17 Quality Control

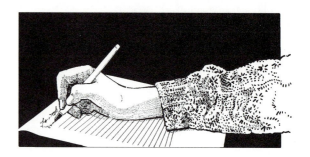

CHAPTER OBJECTIVES

1. To identify seven suggestions that will enhance presentations skills.

2. To identify specific steps presenters can take to implement each of the seven suggestions.

3. To provide encouragement to implement these suggestions for improved presentations.

Successful presenters are always looking for ways to improve their presentations. Top-level presenters are always adjusting and updating their work to produce high-quality presentations.

The quality of a presentation is usually related to the amount of effort and resources the presenter puts into preparation, but other things can be done by presenters to ensure top quality every time. Some presentations fail—even with the very best of preparation and resources.

PRESENTATION ENHANCEMENT SUGGESTIONS

This chapter deals with suggestions to help all presenters give high-quality presentations. The following information will help you improve your overall presentation skills. Perhaps at least one of the following seven suggestions will significantly improve your presentation abilities.

1. Pay attention to the details and eliminate the easy mistakes.
2. Anticipate unexpected opportunities/situations.
3. Make it look easy.
4. Give a little more than the audience expects.
5. Spend appropriate preparation time for anticipated results.
6. Be a nice person.
7. Employ a presentation coach to keep you sharp.

Error is discipline through which we advance.

– William Ellery Channing

Details?

Pay Attention to Details and Eliminate Easy Mistakes

Presenters sometimes fail to pay attention to the details of a presentation. They also forget how easily they can eliminate simple mistakes. Suggestions:

1. Dress one cut above the norm of the group. For example:
   - If you are a man, wear a tie if other men have open shirts.

- If you are a woman, wear a skirt if other women are wearing slacks.
- Wear dressy clothes if everyone else is wearing sports clothes.
- Be cautious in wearing clothes too far away from the norm.
- Check a mirror prior to every presentation to check your appearance. Ask a colleague for help if a mirror is not available.

A tuxedo doesn't help the presenter if it is worn to a presentation at an oil-drilling site where the listeners are dressed in work clothes.

Details!

Consider the postage stamp. Its usefulness consists in the ability to stick to one thing till it gets there.

– Josh Billings

2. Arrive early and have everything ready to go. For example:
   - Place a transparency on the overhead projector before you begin; test the transparency to be sure the projector functions properly; and leave the first slide on the projector so you merely have to turn the projector on to get started when you are ready.

- Place material on the flip chart before you begin.
- Have all equipment set up, tested, and ready to go before the beginning of the meeting.
- Have the tables and chairs neatly and comfortably arranged, with materials already in place where appropriate.

> ## Audiences are usually impressed to see the preliminary signs of a smooth presentation.

---

3. Know the terminology so you can pronounce words and names correctly. For example:
   - Study attendance lists ahead of time so you can be familiar with names and can pronounce them correctly.
   - Identify terms that may be familiar to the audience but not to you, such as Theory Z or total quality management.
4. Call people by appropriate names. For example:
   - Use names appropriately so you don't call a person by the first name where the corporate or societal culture requires titles or surnames.
   - Use names that are common to the audience so you don't call a man Harold when the audience knows him as Hal, or you don't call a woman Elizabeth when the audience knows her as Liz.

> ## One of the best ways to create a good impression is to call a person by the correct name.

---

5. Respect the likes and dislikes of the audience where possible and appropriate. Know the issues that cause the audience to get upset. For example:
   - Don't rent a General Motors vehicle when you present to a Chrysler audience.
   - Don't send materials by U.S. Postal Express when you are working with United Parcel Service.

All great discoveries are made by men whose feelings run ahead of their thinking.

– Charles Parkhurst

- Don't fly Delta when you are presenting to United Airlines.
- Don't call a copy of a document a xeroxed copy when you are working with another company that manufactures copy machines.

An offended audience, intentional or otherwise, greatly reduces the chance a presenter has of succeeding in a presentation.

Anticipate Unexpected Opportunities/Situations

Failures are divided into two classes—those who thought and never did, and those who did and never thought.

– John Charles Salak

Many of the problems presenters have can be eliminated, if presenters think ahead to the presentation and then prepare for situations that might occur. Suggestions:

1. Review previous experiences in presentations to cope with unexpected crises. For example:
   - Carry a backup for every projected visual in case of equipment failure. Be ready to move to an overhead transparency from a computer-driven presentation—or even to a chalkboard or whiteboard—to present your concept if the equipment fails.
   - Have a response ready, even a visual, if you are asked for updates or reports, even though you are not on the agenda. Anticipate what you might be asked to do and plan ahead for it.

One unexpected, unprepared scenario can be labeled a surprise. Two unexpected, unprepared scenarios can be labeled stupidity.

- Be ready with recommendations even though you were asked to bring information without recommendations. Do not offer the recommendation unless requested—but be ready.

- Protect the image of the meeting coordinator by saying something like, "Thank you for giving me time to present my point of view," rather than "I have not been told to expect to speak tonight and I am not really prepared, but I do have some things to say." If you really do not have anything to contribute, simply say, "I don't have anything to add to what has been said," and let the meeting go on.

A problem is a chance for you to do your best.

– Duke Ellington

Most unexpected events can be anticipated and can be corrected before they happen. The others must be handled professionally and with class.

Make It Look Easy

Your listeners need to know you are in charge and are completely at ease. The presentation will probably go well if you appear to be neither disorganized nor nervous (as far as the listeners can tell). Suggestions:

1. Arrive early. Be ready to greet people and visit with them (where appropriate) as they arrive. You are on stage the moment anyone arrives. Look and act appropriately.
2. Make professional comments before, during, and after the presentation. Avoid comments like the following:
   - This has been a very difficult project, and I didn't think I would be ready in time.
   - I didn't think all of you would come.
   - I had planned to finish the XYZ report but couldn't get it ready in time, so I have decided to do this.
   - This is a complicated presentation, but I hope I can get it together so you can understand it.
   - If you have questions, ask my boss. I don't know the answers.
3. Have physical props in place before anyone arrives so you aren't worrying about such things when the audience does arrive.
4. Avoid last-minute rehearsing or looking at the visuals just one more time as people arrive.

If I have ever made any valuable discoveries, it has been owing more to patient attention, than to any other talent.

– Isaac Newton

> **A few simple suggestions can make most pre-sentations seem easy. The audience responds positively to comfortable settings.**

Give More Than the Audience Expects

All audiences arrive at a presentation with expectations in mind. Your research should tell you what those expectations are. Anticipate the expectations and plan for them. Suggestions:

1. Use visuals and lists. Where possible and appropriate, avoid making your presentation with only words in sentences and paragraphs.
2. Provide appropriate handouts.
3. Speak loudly and clearly so everyone can hear and understand. Use a microphone where appropriate.
4. Greet people at the door, both when they arrive and when they leave.
5. Wear a smile and be pleasant.

> **Listeners to a presenter are like customers to a retailer. Listeners and customers respond in many of the same ways. Giving listeners a little more than they expect from a "purchase" keeps them wanting more.**

Spend Appropriate Preparation Time for Appropriate Results

Force, if unassisted by judgment, collapses through its own mass.

– Horace

Presentations can be rated on a scale from one to ten in importance (ten being the most important). Presentation effort can also be rated on that same scale. If the presentation warrants a rating of ten in importance, presentation effort should also warrant a rating of ten. Failure is usually assured where the presenter gives a three to preparation time for a presentation rated at ten.

Another problem occurs where businesspeople are making a lot of presentations. Salespeople and executives often are in this category. One can't spend excessive time in preparing for a presentation because time is a precious commodity. The businessperson carefully guards the use of time. To spend a ten in preparation time, when the outcome will likely result in a four in importance, is a great productivity loss. Suggestions:

Don't expect perfect products unless you are willing to pay for perfection.

– Robert Siegmeister

1. Anticipate the value of the presentation prior to preparation. Then, assign the appropriate preparation time to each presentation.
2. Plan preparation time in your schedule so you can allow appropriate preparation time for each presentation.
3. Identify each presentation's parts that may be used in subsequent presentations and save those parts. These parts include visuals, text material, outlines, and notes. Catalog or file these parts so they can be easily retrieved. Include those parts in appropriate subsequent presentations to save on preparation time.
4. Collect material as you go about your day-to-day duties and as you read. Anticipate your presentation needs and be able to retrieve this material as needed when you prepare presentations.
5. Track your presentations as to your preparation time and the value of the presentation to your work. These are subjective values. Do your best to streamline your preparation time. Then, adjust your preparation time to match the importance of the presentation.

> **Too much time spent on a project is a great loss. The challenge is to know just how much time is the right amount of time. Each presentation has a "critical mass" of preparation time.**

Be a Nice Person

Presenters are finding that audiences respond better to "nice" presenters than to presenters who are not so "nice." Successful presenters find more success when they use techniques used by "nice" people. These successful presenters are powerful, decisive, clear, and dynamic; yet they still can be "nice."

Congruence is an important part of being nice (see Chapter 19, "Congruence"). What you are is what you project when you are presenting. Suggestions:

1. Warm up the face with a smile and interested eyes.
2. Pay attention to people, not things, as you present.
3. Care about what you say.
4. Make positive comments where appropriate, even about negative things.
5. Give credit to others.
6. Recognize the "we" in your presentation to include those who helped, how they helped, and your appreciation for their work.
7. Make constructive comments rather than degrading comments.
8. Tell the truth.
9. Respect your listeners, colleagues, and friends.
10. Keep your humor respectable.
11. Expect the audience to be respectful and to respond to you with respect.

No matter how far you have gone down the wrong road, turn back.

– Turkish Proverb

> **Some businesspeople who do a lot of hiring will tell you that if you have to teach your employees how to be nice, you shouldn't have hired them in the first place. Niceness is one of the most important characteristics for people to have.**

Employ a Presentation Coach to Keep You Sharp

Presenters can learn a lot of lessons from the entertainment industry. Top-level entertainers have one or more coaches who work with them to keep their skills sharp. These coaches are people who know their business and have a strong enough relationship with the presenter that they can tell the presenter what really needs to improve, resulting in the presenter's making changes for the better. Suggestions:

Do not look where you fell, but where you slipped.

– African Proverb

1. Coaches can be found and hired in most medium and large cities where colleges and junior colleges are found. Speech professionals can often function as coaches.

2. Audition a coach as you would an employee. In a sense, a coach is an employee. Take a presentation problem to your coach and have him or her help you with it. If you like the results, use the coach again; if you don't like the results, don't. Contract with your coach one visit at a time in the initial stages.

3. Expect, or even demand, to be videotaped during a coaching session. With a videotape, you can do some of your own coaching after the initial session is over.

4. Videotape yourself often so you can evaluate your own work. Many adjustments can be made within your own walls. A colleague can also help you improve by watching you on a tape.

5. Infrequent visits with a coach are sometimes more effective than a regular, frequent visit—especially in the mature phases of your career. Use your coach when you think you need help or when you have an extreme need to succeed with an important presentation.

Synergy occurs when two people working together can do the work of three or more. A coach will provide a synergistic element to the successful presenter.

Venture not to defend what your judgment doubts of.

– English Saying

CHAPTER SUMMARY

A high-quality presentation requires more than a mechanically sound presentation. Of the millions of business presentations made throughout the world, many are mediocre in nature. Most of those could be dramatically improved with just a little attention to the concepts in this chapter.

You are encouraged to:

- Eliminate the easy mistakes.
- Anticipate unexpected opportunities and situations.
- Make the presentation look easy.
- Provide a bit more than the audience expects.
- Look for ways to streamline your preparation process.
- Spend the appropriate amount of preparation time with each presentation.
- Work at being nice to your listeners.

The above list requires a lifelong effort to complete. You are probably already doing many of these things as you present. Choose one part that needs attention and work on it for a while. Evaluate your progress often and then move to the next item. This procedure will do much to help you improve your presentation technique.

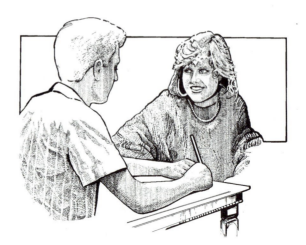

EXERCISES

1. Attend a presentation and note the quality activities surrounding the presentation. Make a list of the activities you notice and discuss the list with a colleague or a friend.

2. Describe three quality activities you would like to incorporate into your presentations to a colleague or a friend.

3. Make a presentation about one of the quality activities you selected in Exercise 2—telling your audience how you plan to improve the quality of your presentations.

4. Develop a tracking document that will allow you to identify and track a quality activity you plan to develop in your presentation routine.

PART III
Delivering the
Presentation

CHAPTER 18 Delivery Choices

CHAPTER OBJECTIVES

1. Choose from four types of presentations.
2. Recognize strengths and weaknesses of each choice.

Now that we have carefully considered how to prepare the *content* of the presentation, we turn our attention to the other half of the presentation—*the presenter.* Understanding the power of the person—the potential contributions of a living, breathing human—helps a presenter prepare effectively.

In Part III, we'll look at techniques that help the presenter deliver an effective presentation. We'll begin by considering what method is best for communicating a presentation clearly.

How should the presentation be given? That question should be answered early in the preparation process. You have five fundamental delivery choices:

1. Extemporaneous
2. Impromptu
3. Manuscript
4. Memorized
5. Combination

Advantages and disadvantages exist for each choice, and different occasions call for different choices. An examination of each choice will help you decide.

EXTEMPORANEOUS DELIVERIES

Extemporaneous means delivering a well-prepared presentation from an outline. Most business presentations are extemporaneous presentations.

The advantages of extemporaneous presentations are that you will probably have:

- Time to prepare with support and visuals.
- The energy of an impromptu presentation and the organization of a memorized presentation.
- A living, breathing, organic delivery.
- Easy-to-remember content when organization is in place.
- Good eye contact with your audience.
- Flexibility.
- An extra measure of allowance for understanding by the audience.

In short, extemporaneous delivery is very useful for most occasions. The secrets to good extemporaneous presentations are what this book is about.

Some people think the only disadvantage of an extemporaneous presentation is that people will ask you to present again and again. Even for the most frightened, that gradually becomes an advantage.

Adaptability is not imitation. It means power of resistance and assimilation.

– Mahatma Gandhi

Mistakes are the portals of discovery.

– James Joyce

The secrets to good extemporaneous presentations are what this book is about.

As I got warmed up, and felt perfectly at home in talk, I heard myself boasting, lying, exaggerating. Oh, not deliberately, far from it. It would be unconvivial and dull to stop and arrest the flow of talk, and speak only after carefully considering whether I was telling the truth.

– Bernard Berenson

The more you present, the better you get.

IMPROMPTU DELIVERIES

Impromptu means presenting on the spur of the moment with little or no preparation.

The advantages of impromptu deliveries are the following:

- You don't have time to be afraid.
- People will understand and forgive some errors.
- The pressure of the moment gives you some energy.

Disadvantages of impromptu deliveries are the following:

- You may have difficulty calling to mind everything you want to say.
- You probably won't have information or visuals with you that could help.

Good organization has saved many an impromptu presentation. The challenge is in using the organization quickly.

Typically, you will not be asked to talk on something about which you know nothing. Usually, the impromptu presentation happens in the board room when the boss says, "Smyth, why don't you tell us about the project you're working on." And there you are, having the moment from your chair to your feet to organize. Doing impromptus well impresses people, even the boss.

Talk not of wasted affection; affection never was wasted.

– Henry Wadsworth Longfellow

Good organization has saved many impromptu presentations.

MANUSCRIPT DELIVERIES

A manuscript presentation is written out and read word for word from start to finish.

The advantages of manuscript deliveries are that you can:
- Say what you want to say.
- Control the format and wording.
- Start and stop at will, restarting where you left off.

The disadvantages are that you:
- Cannot easily adjust the length of the presentation.
- Face the prospect of giving a boring presentation.
- Tend to lose eye contact with the audience.
- May require a great deal of practice if you are to read well with meaning.

Important hints for you to consider when you use a manuscript delivery are the following:
- Practice, practice, practice.
- Make markings on the paper for pauses, meaning, etc.
- Use manuscript delivery for news conferences and for prepared statements.
- Use manuscript delivery when you don't want to be misquoted.

Practice, practice, practice!

I'll be finished in 73 more minutes.

MEMORIZED DELIVERIES

Laughter is not a bad beginning for a friendship, and it is the best ending for one.

– Oscar Wilde

Memorized means written out, committed to memory, and delivered word for word. Two major problems are associated with memorized presentations. First, under pressure, the presenter may have a difficult time remembering. Second, memorization takes time—even for those with so-called "photographic memories."

The advantages of memorized deliveries are the following:
- You can prepare perfectly.
- You can say what you want to say.
- You can prepare the right words and the right format.

The disadvantages of memorized deliveries are as follows:
- You might forget easily. Forgetting even one word can distract you and make the presentation shaky.
- You have little or no flexibility. Once you begin, you can't stop. You destroy audience interaction.

- You may have difficulty making the presentation longer or shorter while you're presenting.
- The presentation may sound "canned."

The demands of a professional stage director reflect an interesting aspect of memorized deliveries. The director might typically prepare for a play by requiring the cast to rehearse for three hours a night for nine weeks. Only then will the director feel secure in the performers' abilities to make a playwright's words truly the performers' own.

You won't have the luxury of that kind of time for most business presentations. And even if you create the words, incomplete memorization will make them stilted and without meaning.

COMBINATION DELIVERIES

Combinations of the four presentation styles are a good idea. Try memorizing a favorite quote or reading a brief excerpt from a book. Short usage of different methods is interesting and gives variety.

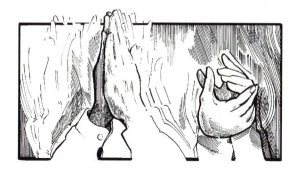

CHAPTER SUMMARY

Five kinds of presentations are possible: extemporaneous, impromptu, manuscript, memorized, and combination. Each has advantages and disadvantages. The most useful in most situations is the extemporaneous presentation, which is what this book is about.

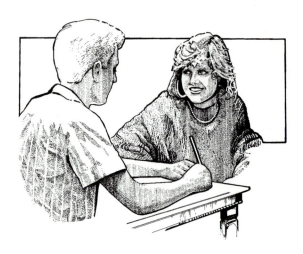

EXERCISES

1. To increase your ability to think on your feet, play a game of charades with friends or coworkers. Divide into two teams and have each team make up slips of paper with the names of movies, books, songs, or people on them. For their own team, members of the team act out the suggestions from the other team. After the game, discuss what you learned about thinking on your feet.

2. A twist on charades is to use the popular drawing game *Pictionary.* A member of each team draws a card at the same time and acts out each of the five words on the card. Whoever finishes first wins. Discuss what you learned. Prepare a list of 10 ways to improve your nonverbal communication.

3. To increase your speed in organization and support, put each one of the following titles (or make up your own) on a card. Then, one at a time, have each prospective presenter draw a card and give a one-minute impromptu presentation on the card's subject.

    *   "A" students make better employees because...
    *   "C" students make better employees because...
    *   Buy foreign made products because...
    *   Buy products made in the Unites States because...

- All states should have mandatory seat-belt laws…
- Minimum wage is a good law because…
- Minimum wage is a bad law because…
- Your convention should be held in (name a city) because…

4. Prepare a five–minute presentation using the extemporaneous style but incorporating memorized and manuscript segments within the presentation.

CHAPTER 19 Congruence

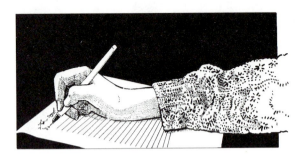

CHAPTER OBJECTIVES

1. Learn what congruence means in presentations.
2. Recognize difficulties with incongruence.
3. Determine ways to improve congruence.

THE MEANING OF CONGRUENCE

What do these synonyms for congruence have to do with presentations? What is it about presentations that needs to be equal, even, appropriate, the same? What needs to fit?

Brainstorming sessions bring up several words to explain congruence—words such as *fit, coordination,* or *equation* surface immediately. The meaning of congruence can easily elude the brainstorming group because members of the group may find themselves grappling for shades of abstractness. Each word seems to contribute something to the meaning sought.

The brainstorming group will usually settle on quite a list. Words such as *agreeing, equal, even, appropriate, the same, coherent, compatible, congenial,* and *consistent* will probably surface.

Congruence?

THE ELEMENTS
OF A CONGRUENT PRESENTATION

Let's examine a presentation's elements that must be *congruent* to make the presentation believable. The list includes the following:

- The message and the body language.
- The presenter's clothes and the occasion.

Shouldn't the message and the occasion also be congruent? What about the body language and the occasion? Other elements include:

- The language and the audience.
- The purpose and the supporting information.
- The visuals and the material.
- The length of the presentation and the time of day.

Certainly, the visuals should be congruent with the audience; and the language *must* be congruent with the material. What we see developing here is a complex interweaving of many presentation elements that must be congruent with many others.

Perhaps the list is endless when we consider the intermixing and complexities of what makes a super presentation. In short, if the presenter is to be credible and successful, *all* elements of the presentation

Being authentic, being actually and precisely what you claim to be…requires that your behavior prove your claim.

– John Hanley

The only meaning a sequence of language has in the real world is the meaning the listener (or reader) understands it to have. Suppose my message is "Here's a rose for you" but you understand me to mean "Here's a frog for you." My intentions are irrelevant to your understanding, and your behavior toward me will be based not on the rose I intended, but on the frog you understood.

– Suzette Haden Elgin

need to *fit* together—they all need to be *congruent*. The task is difficult. A person must be aware of *many* aspects of a presentation at the same time.

Such reasoning is precisely why paying attention to congruence is so important. Grappling with the task shows us a solution is possible. In fact, a solution is obvious. But before we examine what that solution is, let's consider what happens when presentation elements are *incongruent*.

If the presenter is to be credible and successful, all elements of the presentation need to fit together—they all need to be congruent.

POTENTIAL MISUNDERSTANDINGS

Let's examine only the first item in our list. What if the words we speak don't agree with our body language? What if we say out loud, "This is a terrific idea you can support!" while we back away from the audience? The backward movement negates whatever words we say.

What if we present a report on the well-being of the company at the same time we speak in timid tones with our elbows tucked in tightly at our sides—a gesture connoting fear and insecurity? (See Chapter 20, "Body Language.") The audience will doubt the presenter's well-being.

If words and body language disagree, the listener believes the body language (see Chapter 20, "Body Language"). No wonder we come out of some presentations confused. Communication is difficult enough without involving messages that disagree—that are *incongruent!* Successful presentations involve messages that *agree*—that are congruent.

Real glory springs from the silent conquest of ourselves.

– Joseph P. Thompson

If words and body language disagree, the listener will believe the body language.

THE SOLUTION TO INCONGRUENCE

What a person *is* is basic to a credible presentation. Perhaps the solution is as simple as adjusting one's actions. This old adage may be true: "What you are rings so loudly in my ears I can't hear a word you say!" Incongruent acts, such as the colleague who talks behind the back, the boss who is looking for a way to fire the employee, and the dissatisfaction with the job—we could name a multitude of hidden agenda items that affect our congruence as we present.

The simplest way to begin to assure congruence is to *be* what we profess to be.

Congruence!

> ## What a person *is*
> ## is basic to a credible presentation.

In a society that bombards us with advertising about how we're too fat or too old, how we wear the wrong colors, or how we drive the wrong car—all with the end in mind of selling us something else—we can easily forget the miracle of being alive. The stress and the strain of daily living wear grooves of despondency in our patience, our good humor, our health, and our creativity.

From time to time, we should shake ourselves out to remember what it is we *can* do. We can think, make decisions, hope, read, learn, and promise. That is truly an amazing list of abilities. We must remember that.

Speech is the mirror of the soul; as a man speaks, so he is.

– Publius Syrus

> **Our ability to think, make decisions, hope, read, learn, and promise is amazing.**

UNIQUE GIFTS AND THE SHARING OF THEM

If our integrity is intact and if we remember the magnificence of being alive, we are free to be our individual, remarkable selves. Here is where confidence in ourselves and in our abilities can allow us the freedom to be comfortable, warm, giving, at ease, delightful, energetic, informative, knowledgeable, and creative.

In short, we can become the person we are with the friends who bring out the best in us. That's the person we are who presents most comfortably. If we can allow that person the freedom to present, the audience will be interested and will be informed because of the naturalness of the individual.

The most exhausting thing in the world is being insincere.

– Anne Morrow Lindbergh

SUGGESTIONS

So you begin to understand what you are capable of. But how do you instigate such ideas into your life? Assume you're still frightened about the prospects of presenting. Perhaps one or more of the following suggestions will help:

- Use the methods described in this book. Pay attention to both the process of developing the presentation and the delivery parts of the presentation. Both are important.
- Enroll in a presentations workshop. Many companies offer such opportunities. If yours doesn't, check the local college, university, or seminar company.
- Videotape yourself presenting, and then critique the tape honestly. Permit yourself to be a valid critic. Take advantage of what you

like and dislike in others' presentations by objectively watching yourself. The videotape is a great teaching tool. After you've watched yourself on tape a couple of times to get over your embarrassment, not only will you find areas you can improve but also you'll find areas in which you are already terrific. That's a real bonus.

- Take every opportunity to present. Volunteer. Practice. Consider informal opportunities as well. Even engaging in conversations at the water cooler or at the elevator can help you become a strong presenter. Consider what point you want to make, organize your thoughts, and think about what you're doing nonverbally. Learn from your experiences.

- Cultivate the actor in yourself. In this case, you're acting as your best, most-interesting, most-capable self. Though you may be acting at first, you'll become more and more natural, until the process goes beyond acting.

- Change behavior that is undesirable. Now admit it—we all have areas we can improve. You probably already know people suspect you are unprepared, or you know you don't pay enough attention to visual aids, or you have an annoying way of pacing when you're in front of people. Like Benjamin Franklin, we can all improve if we choose to do so. His autobiography explains how he tackled 13 areas he wanted to change. He accomplished them all. We can too.

- Recognize your individual incongruence. Become aware of your incongruent behaviors by direct observation or by listening to a trusted friend.

- Do the best you can with the talents you have. One excellent violin teacher says the world has two kinds of violinists—those who are gifted and excellent and those who quit too soon. We can liken playing the violin to making a presentation. Perhaps the gift is not in making the presentation but in *loving* to make the presentation so we don't quit too soon. We often don't recognize the magnificence of our own talents because we are so comfortable with what we enjoy that things seem commonplace.

- Be yourself. Being told to be yourself probably represents advice you've heard all your life. Naturally, the advice is difficult to follow but is good advice.

- "Just do it." Gradually, you'll feel comfortable. Another Benjamin Franklin concept is, "Persist …[and your] ability to do it increases."

While one person hesitates because he is inferior, the other is busy making mistakes and becoming superior.

– Henry C. Link

*Add to all this the fact that your communication is filtered through such things as how well they can hear or see you, how tired they are, whether they are worried or frightened or sick, how similar factors have affected **your** communication skills, and many other real-world variables.*

– Suzette Haden Elgin

- Emulate someone you admire. Our world is full of admirable people—family, friends, and colleagues. What do you admire about them? Friendliness? Patience? Self-confidence? Focus on that quality; and, with time, you can develop it too.

Pay attention to both the process of developing the presentation and the delivery parts of the presentation.

Take advantage of every opportunity to present.

Cultivate the actor in yourself.

Be yourself.

Genius without education is like silver in the mine.

– Benjamin Franklin

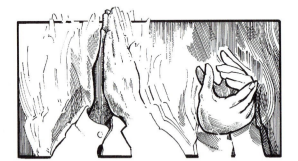

CHAPTER SUMMARY

Congruence is basic to every good presentation. All elements of a presentation need to fit together to support each other. Congruence is best developed when based on integrity, honesty, and self-esteem.

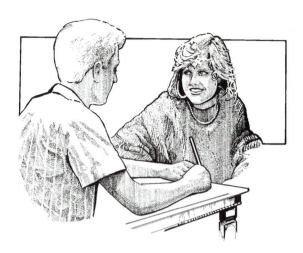

EXERCISES

1. For one day, sincerely smile and thank everyone who serves you—such as taxi drivers, waiters, sales clerks, and others. Report on any changes in behavior you notice in them—or in you.

2. Take a walk and observe anything unusual, beautiful, or interesting on your way. Record your observations when you return home.

3. Talk with a friend or a family member for a period of time and resist any impulse to criticize or be negative. Instead, listen carefully, respond respectfully, and remain calm.

4. Read good literature such as *Les Miserables, To Kill a Mockingbird,* Shakespeare plays, and others. Discuss congruence in major characters such as Jean Valjean, Atticus Finch, or Hamlet.

5. Rent uplifting videos such as *Awakenings, Regarding Henry, Places in the Heart, Shane,* and others. Describe elements of congruence in the videos.

CHAPTER 20 Body Language

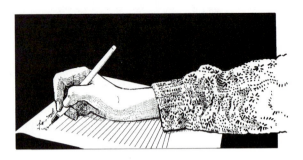

CHAPTER OBJECTIVES

1. Become aware of the power of body language.
2. Learn to send positive nonverbal messages.
3. Practice positive body language during presentations.

Assume you have approached your boss for extended time off. As you emerge from the office, your coworkers quiz you. "What did he say?" You shrug your shoulders, thinking back on the boss's averted eyes, his shoulder turned away from you, and reply, "It wasn't anything he said, actually. It was what I felt."

The communication that takes place outside of what a person says is what we call *nonverbal behavior* or *body language*.

Nonverbal behavior, or body language, is learned culturally. We have all heard of the culture-to-culture embarrassing gestures or behaviors when we miscommunicate in foreign countries. Paying attention to nonverbal behavior is important. However, learning the power of nonverbal behavior in our own culture is vital.

Body language is learned culturally.

Becoming aware of the power of nonverbal communication will increase your effectiveness in presentations. Even conservative estimates maintain that 65 percent of our communication is nonverbal. If the verbal and nonverbal aspects of communication disagree, people will believe the nonverbal.

Do you ever engage yourself in such conversation as the following:

"Why doesn't anybody pay attention to me when I try to enter a conversation? Why won't my colleagues listen to my good ideas? I proposed the solution to our project management, but nobody would do it until Joe proposed the same thing. Why do people fall asleep when I present? They listen to Mary."

Cultivate only the habits that you are willing should master you.

– Elbert Hubbard

I don't understand why they don't listen to me.

By isolating areas of the body, we can examine the power of nonverbal behavior and movement in the communication of our message.

We will look specifically at the face, the arms and hands, the trunk, and the legs and feet.

If the verbal and nonverbal aspects of communication disagree, people will believe the nonverbal.

THE FACE

The most important communication is done by the face. On the face, two areas are of paramount importance.

First are the eyes. In American culture, we make eye contact. As we talk or present, we meet eyes directly; then move away; and then return to eye contact. If listeners are ignored by eye contact, they will retreat from listening. The effective presenter meets the eyes of every listener every few minutes in the small room; and, in a large room, the presenter must meet every area of the room every few minutes. Gracious eye contact is necessary no matter how important or unimportant we think the listener is.

Eye contact is cultural. During a lecture about eye contact, a student from Japan raised his hand and said, "If I had looked at a young woman the way you're telling me to, my parents would have made me marry her." Eye contact in his village was that intrusive.

The second most important area of the face is the mouth. Beyond the words we speak is the power of the warmth, the smile, and the gracious welcome we show to our friends. That's the person we want to be—the natural, charming person we are with our friends. We may have difficulty achieving that role in front of strangers, coworkers, or the boss.

Sometimes facial hair hides the mouth and makes the presenter difficult to understand. It also reduces the warmth.

Some presenters suffer from "lazy lips." Using the lips to articulate properly will aid audience understanding. One lip-reading deaf woman with a young son understood the value of careful articulation. When the son carried on conversations with people, he spoke in normal tones. But whenever he turned to speak specifically with his mother, he lowered his voice to a whisper. He knew that when he whispered, he formed his words on his lips more carefully than when he talked normally. As a result, his mother understood him better.

> ## Problem: Lazy lips?
> ## Try whispering as you practice a presentation to improve the articulation of your lips.

> ## The most important communication is done by the face.

THE ARMS AND HANDS

Think of the arms and hands as your most important visual aids. With them we show size, shape, and placement. As long as the arms and hands have purpose (motivation), they add to—they never detract from—the presentation. In addition, the comfortable use of the arms and hands sends the message that the presenter is at ease, prepared, and competent. For you, that nonverbal message indicates you are at ease, prepared, and competent in other areas of your life.

Think for a moment about your elbows. Pretend you are walking through the forest on a dark night. Pretend you hear something crunching through the leaves and coming up behind you. Do you know what you do with your elbows? (You might have difficulty thinking about elbows at a time like this.) You tuck them to your sides and instinctively try to make yourself as small as possible. You are afraid, and your fear shows in your elbows.

Interestingly enough, your elbows are what show you're afraid when you present as well. Work in ways to make fully extended gestures to a visual, an overhead, or a screen. Full, confident gestures put you in charge of the presentation and the information. They make you appear unafraid.

Imagine yourself without elbows!

> **Think of the arms and hands as your most important visual aids.**

THE TRUNK

Another area of the body you must be aware of is the trunk—without the head, arms, or legs. The trunk is the area of the body where we show *attitude*.

Pretend you and a friend are standing face to face talking when someone you don't want to talk to approaches. Do you know what you and your friend do with the trunks of your bodies? Right. You turn your shoulders away from the person approaching and hope the message will get across that you don't want to speak. You do the opposite when you want to speak with the person. You open your shoulders toward the person and welcome him or her to the group.

The area of the body where we show attitude is the trunk.

An important area of the trunk is what is called the "honor zone." The honor zone is located in the upper chest area. You communicate power by keeping the honor zone high and confident (sort of like when your mother told you to "Stand up straight!" or "Put your shoulders back!").

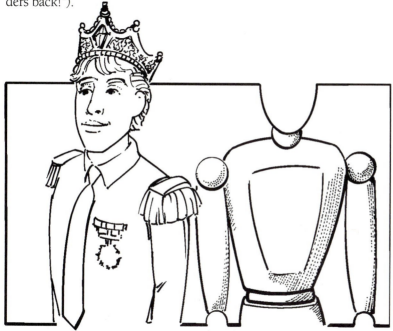

Listeners look to the honor zone for the presenter's authority.

When you present, you are always the king.

Here is a way to view the trunk in relation to the honor zone. Suppose a stage director told you to walk across the stage like a king. You know how to do that—your movement becomes regal, powerful, and confident. (You also know how to walk across like a downtrodden peasant. Your shoulders sag, and your head lowers.) Remember—when you present, you are always the king.

THE LEGS AND FEET

The chains of habit are too weak to be felt until they are too strong to be broken.

– Samuel Johnson

When presenting, keep your weight evenly balanced on both feet. Avoid the desire to place all your weight on one foot either to one side or in back of the other foot. Both uneven stances give a nonverbal message of retreat or lack of preparation. In addition, shift the evenly distributed weight a bit forward to the balls of the feet. The resulting body carriage will make the presenter appear alert, ready, and caring. In addition, you can more easily move when the weight is already forward on the feet.

Though we can simply say you should keep your feet under you, consider the things in a presentation room that get in your way—cords from the overhead projector, legs on the tripod of the flip chart, the table legs, or the chairs. You must realize the importance of keeping your movement area as free from conflict as possible.

MOVEMENT

Too much movement causes distraction because observers concentrate on a presenter's dancing feet. Too little movement is boring. The key, again, is moving for a purpose. Try moving at a transition point in the presentation, or set the visual aids up on different sides of the room so you have to move back and forth to use them.

Move for a purpose.

PERSONAL SPACE

People carry a bubble of a certain size around them. This bubble is culturally created. This bubble is the space we maintain between us and other people. We allow people—our own loved ones, children, and perhaps animals—to break into the bubble with permission.

People in the United States have fairly large personal bubbles compared to the rest of the world. And people in the western United States have larger personal bubbles than people living in the eastern United States. Perhaps that is because of the wide open spaces in the West.

Knowing that personal space exists helps us develop power to use it. When you are alone in an elevator, where do you stand? Probably in the middle. How does this change when another person enters? You probably divide the space in half. No one teaches us where to stand in an elevator. We learn it culturally.

The following behaviors are best avoided:

- The Superman pose. Both hands are on the hips, and the feet are spread apart—a position indicating the presenter is much more powerful than anyone in the audience.
- The fig-leaf stance. Both arms are in the front of the body with the hands clasped at the end of the extended arms—a position that renders the arms and hands useless as part of the presentation.
- Bonaparte's retreat. One hand is across the front and is secured against the chest, thereby hiding part of the honor zone and rendering the arm and hand a useless part of the presentation— a position suggesting the presenter has more power than the audience has.
- The stakeout stance. Also called the reverse fig leaf. Both arms are behind the back with the hands clasped—a position indicating the presenter has no use for the arms and hands, so they are best not to be noticed.
- The "Jingle Bells" stance. One or both hands are in the pockets containing items that jingle, such as keys, coins, or other metal objects. The presenter's hands "work" the objects so the objects jingle constantly and distract the audience.
- The scaredy-cat stance. The toes are pointed inward, the knees are together, the shoulders are down, and the arms and hands are across the chest—a position that indicates the presenter is scared to death and may not survive the presentation. No honor zone is showing.

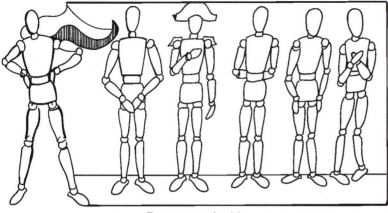

Postures to Avoid.

AUTISTIC BEHAVIORS

Any behavior that calls attention to itself, instead of to what the gesture or behavior represents, can be termed an *autistic behavior.* Autistic behaviors are dysfunctional because of their masking nature. Gestures, behaviors, and nonverbal communication should all be used to support, to explain, and to clarify—not just to exist for themselves. They should work together like a marvelous instrument to achieve the whole.

Action, to be effective, must be directed to clearly conceived ends.

– Jawaharlal Nehru

Some typical autistic behaviors to avoid are the following:

- Tapping the fingers.
- Twiddling the thumbs.
- Cracking the knuckles.
- Interlacing and unlacing the fingers.
- Making tapping noise with pen, pointer, or foot.
- Shrugging the shoulders.
- Tugging at clothing.
- Pacing to and fro.
- Scratching body parts.
- Pulling the ears.
- Twitching the nose and eyeglasses.
- Furrowing the brow.
- Licking, biting, or pursing the lips.
- Noticeably blinking the eyelids.
- Picking the nose.
- Stroking the chin.
- Playing with items in a pocket or with jewelry.

CHAPTER SUMMARY

Everyone learns naturally to communicate nonverbally. By realizing the power of communication in the face, the hands and arms, the trunk, and the legs and feet, the presenter can manage nonverbal communication effectively. The use of movement, the recognition of personal space, and the avoidance of autistic behaviors increase presentation quality.

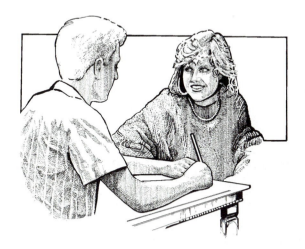

EXERCISES

1. Play charades with family or friends. List and explain 10 things you learned about nonverbal communication.

2. Notice nonverbal communication of those around you and "mirror" movement to watch the effect on other people. Discuss the effects of noticing and mirroring.

3. Do a one- or two-minute pantomime of some familiar action. Try communicating a sport, preparing food, or getting dressed in the morning. After you finish, have others in the room guess what you were doing and give feedback about the specific movements.

4. Watch Marcel Marceau videotapes. Identify techniques for clear body language.

5. Give a three-minute business presentation focusing on using your arms and hands as visual aids. Use them to show size, shape, and direction. Be sure to include at least one gesture with full arm extension.

CHAPTER 21 Voice

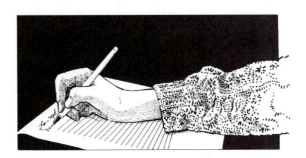

CHAPTER OBJECTIVES

1. Recognize the importance of correct vocal production.
2. Manage vocal variables advantageously.
3. Discover remedies for vocal problems.

Do you remember how you felt about your voice the first time you heard it on a tape recorder? You probably didn't like it. Perhaps you discovered that strange as your voice sounded, it wasn't really all that bad. But perhaps you could use some improvement.

We just seem to let voice and vocal production *happen*, unless we become interested in singing or other performances. A little attention to vocal production can work miracles in how we sound in a presentation.

Two areas of voice matter. They are vocal production and the vocal variables. By focusing on these two areas, everyone can improve.

No, I did not inhale a helium balloon!

A little attention to vocal production can work miracles in how we sound in a presentation.

VOCAL PRODUCTION

Two muscles involved in vocal production can be developed to enhance the voice. As with any other muscle, proper exercise improves performance. First, let's look at the diaphragm muscle. Then, we'll consider the larynx.

Natural abilities are like natural plants that need pruning by study.

– Francis Bacon

Diaphragm Muscle

The diaphragm muscle is a sheaf of muscle lying between the stomach and the lungs. The diaphragm muscle is what makes us breathe. By increasing the strength and flexibility of the diaphragm muscle, we can remedy several vocal problems.

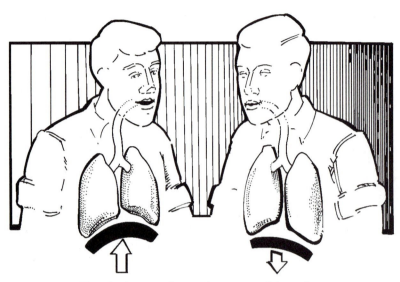

The diaphragm directs the power of the voice.

Problem: Whispery, crackly, or weak voice? Solution: For one minute a day for two weeks, say "Ha, ha, ha," or "Ho, ho, ho!" You can feel if the right muscle is being exercised by placing the hand just below the rib cage while doing this exercise. Proper diaphragm involvement should bounce the hand.

Larynx

The larynx is in the throat. You can find the location by placing two fingers against the throat and humming. Where the "buzzing" is felt is the location of the larynx. The larynx itself is a section of throat cartilage that contains the vocal chords or bands. It looks like the illustration on the following page.

Courage is grace under pressure.

– Ernest Hemingway

The vocal bands come out from the sides and vibrate together much like the top of a balloon does when the air is allowed to escape. Proper vocal production requires the larynx area to remain relaxed and comfortable. Because that's hard to do under the stress of presentation, the exercise to overcome a tense edge to the voice is useful.

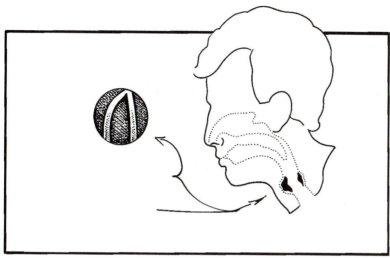

The larynx contains the vocal chords.

Problem: Tense edge to voice?
Solution: Pretend you have a tennis ball at the back of the throat. Or drop the jaw like just before a yawn. For one minute a day for two weeks, speak or read aloud in a relaxed, full-throated voice. You become in command of the muscle that governs the larynx area of the throat.

In addition to working with *how* the voice is produced, we can work with some simple variables to improve how the voice sounds.

VOCAL VARIABLES

Your voice has three characteristics that can normally be changed any time you want. These three are *pitch, volume,* and *rate*. People who choose to take advantage of these variables improve the interest of their listeners. We teach the variables here precisely because achieving variety in pitch, volume, and rate is much more interesting than speaking without such variety.

No matter how well dressed you are, no matter how elegantly you sit and stand and move, if your voice is unpleasant your communication is not going to be as effective and satisfactory as it ought to be. And unless you can control your voice quality, you risk losing control of the messages you're transmitting to others.

– Suzette Haden Elgin

> # You can change three things about your voice any time you want. They are pitch, volume, and rate.

Pitch

Some people, especially some macho-type men or some women with high-pitched voices, think they have found the ultimate four notes in which to speak. They use only those notes and rapidly bore the rest of the world with their monotone, flat speech. Sounds, words, and ideas are greatly improved when we use several notes in the middle and add occasional highs and lows.

> # Problem: Monotone voice?
> # Solution: For one minute a day for two weeks, read aloud while changing the voice from as high as it can go to as low as it can go over and over again. This exercise will put you in charge of a throat muscle that governs pitch. By exercising the muscle, you can train it to react properly.

Talk happiness. The world is sad enough without your woe. No path is wholly rough.

– Ella Wheeler Wilcox

Studies indicate that middle to lower tones test better in the board room for both men and women. Some women especially need to work on lowering their voices. Higher "teen-age" voices used by some people well into adulthood tend to lower credibility. One man had a beautiful tenor voice but wanted to sing bass. Over the course of 10 years, he achieved his goal by lowering his voice an entire octave. He lost nothing in the tenor range and gained an octave in the baritone range.

Successful presenters use a variety of vocal tones.

Problem: Voice too high?
Solution: For one minute a day for two weeks, read aloud from the middle to lower tones over and over again. We're working on the length of the muscle that governs pitch. This exercise will need to be repeated at intervals to achieve consistently lower tones.

Women tend to pitch their voices higher than men do, and this is a strike against them in almost every language interaction. Not because there is anything inherently wrong with high-pitched voices, but because AME (American Mainstream English) speakers associate them with children.

– Suzette Haden Elgin

Studies indicate that middle to lower tones test better in the board room.

Volume

The first responsibility you have as a presenter is to be heard. No amount of valuable information makes up for speaking too quietly or indistinctly for listeners to hear. The opposite problem is also difficult. The too-loud voice is irritating. The most useful volume uses a variety of loud and soft in the comfort range of the listeners.

Problem: The room is too big or the micro-phone system stops working?
Solution: Avoid trying to shout more loudly from the throat. The throat will become sore, and the voice will become hoarse very quickly. The secret to a louder voice is using the diaphragm muscle to support the extra effort needed in the voice. Try the "ha, ha, ha" or "ho, ho, ho" exercise to strengthen the diaphragm muscle. (See drawing of diaphragm muscle on page 194.)

Your first responsibility as a presenter is to be heard.

Rate

Variety in rate is the third vocal variable that increases interest in the listener. Talking very rapidly all the time is as wearing as talking slowly all the time. Listeners much prefer some differences in the rate of speech. Rate is also the variable that allows you, as a presenter, to signal the listener which words are most important in a presentation.

The most important element of rate is the use of the pause. Entire meanings can be changed by where the pause is placed.

Problem: How do I make clear what I mean?
Solution: When determining what is important
in a sentence, consider the differences in
meanings simply by where the pause is placed.
I / never said you mugged him.
I never / said you mugged him.
I never said / you mugged him.
I never said you / mugged him.
I never said you mugged / him.

Listeners react positively to some differences
in the rate of speech.

By paying close attention to both vocal production and the three vocal variables, you can quickly improve presentation skills. In addition, exercising vocal areas for a period of time will make lasting improvements.

The voice is a second face.

– Gerand Bauer

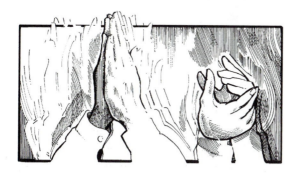

CHAPTER SUMMARY

Attention to vocal production by strengthening the diaphragm muscle and relaxing the larynx improves the sound of the voice. In addition, using variety in pitch, volume, and rate increases effectiveness and encourages listeners to pay attention.

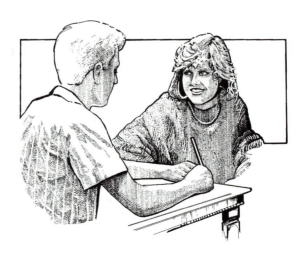

EXERCISES

1. Read aloud into a tape recorder or use a video recorder as you read the following poem. As you play back the recording, look for three things you do well and three things you can improve. Then try the activity again—working on one area at a time for improvement.

Jabberwocky

by Lewis Carroll

Twas brillig, and the slithy toves
     Did gyre and gimble in the wabe;
All mimsy were the borogoves,
     And the mome raths outgrabe.
"Beware the Jabberwock, my son!
     The jaws that bite, the claws that catch!
Beware the Jubjub bird, and shun
     The frumious Bandersnatch!"

He took his vorpal sword in hand;
     Long time the manxome foe he sought—
So rested he by the Tumtum tree,
     And stood awhile in thought.

And as in uffish thought he stood,
     The Jabberwock, with eyes of flame,
Came whiffling through the tulgey wood,
     And burbled as it came!

One, two! One, two! And through and through
            The vorpal blade went snicker-snack
He left it dead, and with its head
            He went galumphing back.

"And hast thou slain the Jabberwock?
            Come to my arms, my beamish boy!
O frabjous day! Callooh! Callay!"
            He chortled in his joy.

2. Record a newscaster such as Peter Jennings, Dan Rather, Diane
    Sawyer, Connie Chung, or any of the men or women newscast-
    ers on television or radio. Play the tape over a few times listening
    for vocal dynamics. Then, begin to speak along with the tape.
    Remember, you are trying to learn to *hear* vocal pitch, rate, and
    volume as well as pronunciation.

3. Practice telling a scary story or a funny story into a tape recorder
    or on a videotape. When you listen to yourself, notice what you
    do naturally to set up the dramatic moments and the important
    elements. Now use that same naturalness when you speak in
    other situations.

4. Record yourself on a tape recorder or on a videotape as you read
    aloud from a child's book by Dr. Seuss such as *Horton Hatches the
    Egg* or *Green Eggs and Ham.* Or read a poem aloud from one of
    Shel Silverstein's books like *Where the Sidewalk Ends* or *A Light in
    the Attic.* Focus on meaning.

5. Sing in the shower to practice vocal variables.

CHAPTER 22 # Diction, Language, and Grammar

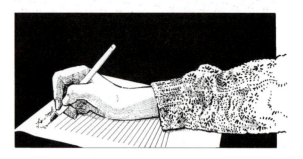

CHAPTER OBJECTIVES

1. Understand the nature of good speech.
2. Learn to pay attention to regionalisms and to correct them.
3. Discover common pronunciation problems.

We are judged by our speech. The quickest indicator of education or intelligence is proven to be speech. Logic tells us that speech involves more than education or intelligence, yet listeners often judge a presenter's education or intelligence by pronunciation and grammar standards.

THE NATURE OF GOOD SPEECH

Good speech doesn't call attention to itself. Good speech includes correct pronunciation as well as correct grammar. Good speech may be different in various areas of the country, but a clear standard is what we call middle American radio speech.

I'll be speakin and teachin, and you'll be learning.

Travelers all over the country can tune in to radio or television stations in any market and find the same level of good speech. Professional announcers can go into any market in the country and find that the same standard of speech prevails.

One professor facetiously tells her undergraduate students that a few selected words are "dead giveaways" to level of education. The professor then tells her students that if they want to show people their college education has been worthwhile, the students can do so by accurately pronouncing those few selected words.

The quickest indicator of education or intelligence is speech.

One of the words is *et cetera*. People often say *ek cetera*.

Another word is *worcestershire*, like the sauce. When students know the syllables are broken between *worce* and *ster,* the students remember the pronunciation much better.

A third word is the pronunciation of the German writer's name, *Goethe*. Young people who have read only the name, of course, say *go-eth*. The *o* followed by an *e* in German has the same sound as *ö*. That sound is made by forming an *e* with the mouth and then closing

What we say is important...for in most cases the mouth speaks what the heart is full of.

– Jim Beggs

lips around the *e* into an *o*. Although that isn't a sound we have in English, sometimes people think it sounds like *Gerta*. That's closer than *go-eth*.

A consultant found herself in Philadelphia working on sales presentations with a national car company. As she watched the workshop participants enter the room, she noticed a tall, blond young man with an attractive air of confidence about him. She thought to herself, "This company surely knows how to hire sales managers. I would buy from him in a minute!"

Then the young man began speaking. His thick Philadelphia accent would be useful in Philadelphia only. After he was videotaped for the first time and viewed the tape, he said to the consultant, "I sound like Rocky Balboa."

The consultant was surprised to discover the young man really hadn't known how he sounded. He and the consultant talked about immediate exercises and long-term exercises. In the three days they worked together, he made an excellent beginning on improving his pronunciation. But first he had to hear what he sounded like.

No matter what his other skills were, that young man was maximally useful to the company only in Philadelphia, until he changed his speech.

How do you sound? Can people understand you? Are you using words correctly?

In our speaking, we all have "regionalisms" to some degree. As we grow up, we speak like the people around us speak.

This fact was made abundantly clear to a young college student when she first went away to college as a freshman. She was only 200 miles away from home, but her roommates insisted she had an accent. They laughed when she talked about the opposite of south being *narth* or when she talked about setting the table with spoons and *farks*. The student had difficulty believing her roommates.

Five weeks later, she went home for the weekend. Amazingly, she discovered her parents had begun to say *narth* and *fark* while she was away at college.

One of the roommates who found the student's accent so out of the ordinary was Marci, who was from Massachusetts. During November of the students' freshman year, John F. Kennedy was elected President. When Marci returned to school from Christmas vacation, she had lost every *r* in her vocabulary. At one point, she announced to the whole dorm that everyone was going to have a *pahty*. Perhaps you have noticed how some people let their regionalisms show after

Yes, the more you wish to describe a Universal, the more minutely and truthfully you must describe a Particular.

– Brenda Ueland

During World War II, the Civil Defense authorities had posters printed which read: "Illumination must be extinguished when premises are vacated." When he saw these signs, President Franklin Roosevelt exclaimed, "Damn, why can't they say 'Put out the lights when you leave'"?

– Dormann

President Carter or President Clinton was elected. The southern drawl is much more popular with a southern president in the White House.

For our purposes here, let's consider pronunciation, enunciation, and diction elements of the same thing. They all refer to the clarity and accuracy of our speech.

Proper speech is powerful!

Good speech doesn't call attention to itself.

CHANGES IN USAGE OR PRONUNCIATION

If we lived in France. we would know that French rules are made by the Académie Française, a body of 40 literary figures who make decisions about correct French usage and grammar. However, citizens of the United States have no such body. By observing what has happened to English since the United States and England parted, we know

I would make boys all learn English; and then I would let the clever ones learn Latin as an honor and Greek as a treat. But the only thing I would whip them for is not knowing English. I would whip them hard for that.

– Winston Churchill

changes are made. But how? We talk about American English being changed by usage. Who decides when those changes occur?

In the United States, about 60 different editions of dictionaries are printed. Each dictionary is typically revised every five years or so. So, in any given year, several editions are under revision. The publishers of dictionaries survey the American people about usage. When a certain percentage reports that meanings have changed, a new word has been coined, or pronunciation has changed, the dictionaries are updated.

As a result, dictionaries at different levels of revision sometimes don't agree with each other. For example, look at the word *nuclear*. The spelling suggests that *nuclear* is pronounced *nu-cle-ar*. However, during the Carter administration, dictionaries began publishing one pronunciation choice as *nu-kju-lar*. That's an illustration of how pronunciation changes.

> ## Who decides when changes in American English should occur?

CAUSES OF POOR SPEECH

The major cause of poor speech is our mimicking of the speech around us. This became clear to one American communication professor when some friends of hers moved to London with their three-year-old daughter, Chrissy. There, Chrissy attended nursery school with English children her age. No matter how much American English she heard at home, her three hours a day hearing British English developed a delightful British accent in the little girl.

When the family visited the American professor over the holidays, the professor was amazed that this little British-accented child belonged to her American parents.

When Chrissy was in kindergarten, the family moved home to Virginia. Chrissy took about six weeks to lose every semblance of British pronunciation. That shows the power of peer pressure.

> ## The major cause of poor speech is our mimicking of the speech around us.

REMEDIES FOR POOR SPEECH

Like the young automobile sales manager in Philadelphia, most people willingly adjust their poor speech when they discover it. The trick is discovering they have poor speech habits. First, the speaker has to hear the poor speech. By looking as some common mispronunciations, we can discover some possible problems with our own speech.

Probably the most common error is lazy articulation.

- Leaving syllables out—*probly* instead of *probably*, *salry* instead of *salary*.
- Lazily pushing two words together—*doncha, cantcha* instead of *don't you, can't you*.
- Leaving endings off words—*doin', bein', goin'*.
- Changing sounds—*gonna, gimme*, instead of *going to, give me*.
- Leaving sounds out—for *towel* saying *tal*, omitting the *t* in *postpone* or the *g* in *recognize*.

Another error is using the wrong pronunciation. This error often occurs in words we've only read without connecting their pronunciation with the word we probably already know.

- Many students have stumbled on *subtle* and included the *b* when reading aloud.
- Another young reader knew the word *deny* perfectly well but pronounced it *denny* when he read it aloud.

Sometimes, we have learned the word the less-preferred way in our section of the country. As a child, one communication specialist learned the following nursery rhyme:

> There was a little girl, with a little curl right in the middle of her *forehead*.
>
> When she was good she was very very good, but when she was bad she was *horrid*.

The specialist didn't discover until she was an adult that *horrid* and *forehead* rhyme! In the section of the country where the specialist was raised, the words didn't rhyme. A similar thing happened with the word *toward*. The specialist learned to pronounce it with two syllables. Later, she discovered the preferred pronunciation has one syllable, *tord*, and that people actually said *toward* that way.

The specialist observed that when she began pronouncing *forehead* and *toward* correctly, she heard people pronouncing them the new way all over the place. With amazement, she observed people often do not hear correctly until their attention is drawn to correct pronunciation.

WEASEL WORDS

Many presenters use phrases like "I would like to tell you," "Perhaps you'll see the value…," and "It seems possible that…" We call these "weasel words," because they communicate a lack of confidence and a sense of indecisiveness. Weasel words like *maybe, perhaps,* and *almost* weaken statements.

Unless we have a compelling reason to express indecision, we should avoid weasel words. Listeners respond more positively to confident, direct statements like "I will explain…" and "You'll discover that…" and "We suggest…"

CORRECT GRAMMAR

Punctuation, to most people, is a set of arbitrary and rather silly rules you find in printer's style books and in the back pages of school grammars. Few people realize that it is the most important single device for making things easier to read.

– Rudolf Flesch

The process of learning correct grammar is far larger than we can work with in this text. However, we must emphasize the importance of correct grammar. Grammar mistakes hold us back. Reasonable people think that if we easily make grammatical errors, we easily make other errors.

Grammar matters. If you've slipped through your educational process detesting grammar study and missing corrections you might have made easily, get your hands on a simple grammar book and begin to discover where you make your errors.

> ## Grammar mistakes hold us back.

CHAPTER SUMMARY

Good speech improves communication. Presenters can learn the nature of good speech and absorb it into their own work by knowing some causes of poor speech and learning ways to remedy them. Mispronunciation, lazy pronunciation, regionalisms, and weasel words can all be improved by the presenter's paying attention to and using correct speech.

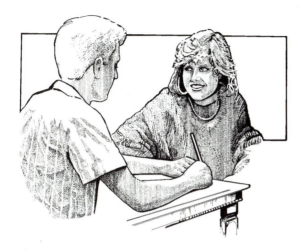

EXERCISES

1. To improve articulation, do tongue twisters. One minute a day for two weeks will make a significant difference. Try these:
    *   Peter Piper picked a peck of pickled peppers,
        A peck of pickled peppers did Peter Piper pick.
        If Peter Piper picked a peck of pickled peppers,
        How many pickled peppers did Peter Piper pick?
    *   A big black bug bit a big black bear;
        Where's the big black bear that the big black bug bit?
    *   The trustees decreed that seniors be free from fees.
    *   A lusty lady loved a little lawyer and longed to lure him from his lonely laboratory.

2. Listen carefully to radio and television announcers. Critique the voices and pronunciations you hear. Why are the presentations of some announcers more pleasing to you than the presentations of others? Identify an area or two that needs improvement in your own speech.

3. Record your own voice by reading some material from the newspaper or from a book. Listen carefully for sounds you need to improve. Repeat this exercise in two-week intervals, reading the same material and comparing each time to the previous work.

4. Pronounce the following words. Then check your pronunciations with the preferred pronunciations.

indictment	\in-'dɪt-mənt\
qualm	\kwäm\
vineyard	\'vin-yərd\
heinous	\'hA-nəs\
ribald	\'rib-bəld\
route	\'rʊt\
quay	\'kE, 'kwA\
often	\'ôf-ən\
hiccough	\'hi-kəp\
data	\'dA-tə\
bade	\'bad, 'bAd\
escape	\is-'kAp'\
pique	\'pEk\
extraordinary	\ik-'stror-dn-er-E\
epistle	\i-'pi-səl\
awry	\ə-'rɪ\
blatant	\'blA-tnt\
err	\'er\
alias	\'A-lE-əs\
mischievous	\'mis-chə-vəs\
maniacal	\mə-'nɪ-ə-kəl\
genuine	\'jen-yə-wən\
forehead	\'fär-əd\
creek	\krEk\
museum	\myʊ-'zE-əm\
ophthalmologist	\äf-thə-'mä-lə-jist\
succinct	\sək-'singt'\
regime	\rA-'zhEm\
thyme	\'tɪm\
penalize	\'pE-nl-ɪz\
schedule	\'ske-jʊl\

picture	\'pik-chər\
suite	\swɛt\
nuclear	\'nU-klE-ər\
abdomen	\'ab-də-mən\
toward	\tɔrd\
poignant	\'pôi-nyənt\
coupon	\'k(y)U-pän\
which	\hwich\
larynx	\'lar-iə(k)s\

\ä\	cot, cart
\ə\	abut
\ô\	law
\ôi\	boy
\A\	ace
\E\	easy
\I\	ice
\o\	go
\U\	loot

Pronunciations taken from *Merriam Webster's Tenth New Collegiate Dictionary,* 1993.

5. Begin a list of words you hear people say differently from the way you say them. Look them up in the dictionary. Commit to saying them the way the dictionary suggests.

CHAPTER 23 Interpretation

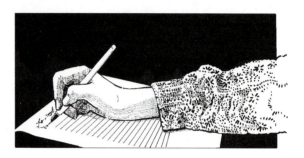

CHAPTER OBJECTIVES

1. Discover the power of interpretation.
2. Develop skills of interpretation.
3. Manage interpretation choices.

Often, a presenter protests by saying, "But I shouldn't smile in this presentation. Business is serious!" And otherwise animated, interesting people often take on a dull, monotone voice as soon as they begin to present.

Why are some presentations yawningly dull and others imaginatively alive? The skill is in the *interpretation*.

UNDERSTANDING INTERPRETATION

Interpretation is the meaning we give the words we speak. The meaning and mood of a good presentation carry energy, motivation, caring—that is, *interpretation*. Such effective oral expression is the result of clear thinking. Clear thinking expresses ideas, thoughts, words, and feelings in imaginative and interesting ways. Understanding the skill of interpretation can improve any presentation.

Well...I uh...well...uh...I'm really excited...uh...about this.

> # Interpretation is the meaning we give the words we speak.

DEVELOPING INTERPRETATION

We should say words with the meaning we've assigned them. For example, easy words to give meaning to are those that intrinsically have onomatopoeia. These words have their meaning built in. *Buzz,* for example, sounds like a buzz. *Fish* sounds slick and shiny. And, to some people, *chrysanthemum* sounds round and many-petaled.

A bit more challenging are the words that have several meanings.

Originality is nothing but judicious imitation.

– Voltaire

We have to convey the meaning by the interpretation of the word. Let's use *hot,* for example.

If your friend squirms and sweats uncomfortably and tells you, "It's hot!," you'll know your friend means the weather. But if your friend touches something and recoils sharply and exclaims, "It's hot!," you'll know your friend means the temperature of something. If your friend smiles and admiringly explains, "It's hot!," you'll know your friend approves of something, that it's neat, and, yes, that it's "cool." (What a language we speak when opposites can mean the same thing!)

So a presenter's interpretation of the word lets the listener understand what the presenter means. Now, let's say a coworker wants to talk to you about an automobile in the parking lot and, with a completely passionless face and unimaginative voice, says to you, "There's a hot car in the parking lot." What do you think your coworker means? Without your coworker's help, you have several guesses about what is being conveyed. Which sentence explains the meaning?

Nobody can be exactly like me. Sometimes even I have trouble doing it.

– Tallulah Bankhead

- The sun has been merciless all day, so there's a hot car in the parking lot.
- Did you see that red sports car out there? For once there's a hot car in the parking lot.
- The police are swarming all over the place. That must mean there's a hot car in the parking lot.

If a presenter gives meaning to the word, he or she interprets; and the listener will probably understand.

Now that's a hot car!

> # A presenter's interpretation of the word lets you understand what the presenter means.

Most difficult and probably most important is the meaning we *should* give to important words. For example, assume you are presenting a new idea to your boss. If you tell your boss with a straight face and a boring voice that you have a "terrific idea," your boss probably won't believe you. But if you give the word terrific "energy" (caring, imagination, and meaning)—*interpretation*—your boss may be interested enough to continue to listen.

Words, like glasses, obscure everything they do not make clear.

– Joseph Joubert

Another part of interpretation skill is learning to "point" up the important word. *Point* means to emphasize or stress—*interpret*—what you want listeners to understand by which words you choose to make the most important. Consider the following sentences and the different meanings given by which words are pointed up.

> The *swans* sail near the boats on the muddy river.
> The swans *sail* near the boats on the muddy river.
> The swans sail *near* the boats on the muddy river.
> The swans sail near the *boats* on the muddy river.
> The swans sail near the boats on the *muddy* river.
> The swans sail near the boats on the muddy *river.*

Much pointing up comes naturally. We can improve our natural interpretation by the meaning, caring, and emphasis we give to the words we want to make clear.

> # *Point* means to emphasize or stress (interpret) what you want listeners to understand by which words you choose to make the most important.

Good writing offers opportunity to interpret and to create mood. The writing is so well done that interpretation is easy to do. Consider Edgar Allen Poe's work. Here is the first sentence from *The Fall of the House of Usher.*

During the whole of a dull, dark and soundless day in the autumn of the year, when the clouds hung oppressively low in the heavens, I had been passing alone, on horseback, through a singularly dreary tract of country; and at length found myself, as the shades of evening drew on, within view of the melancholy House of Usher.

Those words almost force you to read them with the meaning they carry.

MAKING INTERPRETATION EASY

Words, like fine flowers, have their colours too.

– Ernest Rhys

In each of us are places we have never gone. Only by pressing the limits do you ever find them.

– Joyce Brothers

So interpretation paints pictures in other people's minds. Such interpretation increases interest, clarity, and meaning in whatever you present. Clearly, the task becomes easy if you are interested in your subject and if you care about what you talk about.

But what if you don't care about the subject? What if you even have to present something you disagree with—a change in company policy, for example? How can you give an effective presentation then? You simply must find something you do agree with or care about—perhaps supporting the boss, keeping your job, or learning from the difficult situation—that will enable you to interpret carefully.

> # Interpretation paints pictures in other people's minds.

CHAPTER SUMMARY

Interpretation makes the words we speak more understandable to the listener. Interesting and otherwise clear personalities can be hampered by the pressure of public presentation. Being aware of interpretation skills can enable the presenter to manage meaning more productively.

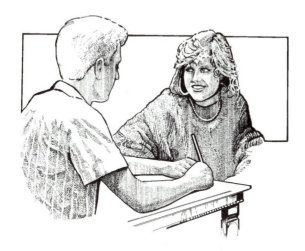

EXERCISES

1. Read aloud the following first paragraph of Charles Dickens's *A Tale of Two Cities*. Pay attention to the meaning of the words. Give meaning to the words as you read.

    > *It was the best of times, it was the worst of times, it was the age of wisdom, it was the age of foolishness, it was the epoch of belief, it was the epoch of incredulity, it was the season of Light, it was the season of Darkness, it was the spring of hope, it was the winter of despair, we had everything before us, we had nothing before us, we were all going direct to Heaven, we were all going direct the other way—in short, the period was so far like the present period, that some of its noisiest authorities insisted on its being received, for good or for evil, in the superlative degree of comparison only.*

2. Write about something that happened to you where you felt an extreme of emotion—such as fear or anger. Record how you felt when the original event happened, and then try to feel that way again.

3. To help yourself become aware of the imagery in language, focus on language that triggers the senses. For example, on videotape, describe to a friend the mountains, a sunset, the ocean, a child, an animal, or something else you have seen. Be sure to *see* in your own mind what you describe.

4. Practice the same exercise described in No. 3, but focus on an intense experience with sound. For example, describe the sound of a waterfall, traffic congestions, a symphony, a crying baby, or crowd noise at a basketball game.

5. Now continue the exercise described in No. 3, but focus on intense experiences with taste, smell, or touch.

6. Read *An Actor Prepares* by Konstantin Stanislavski.

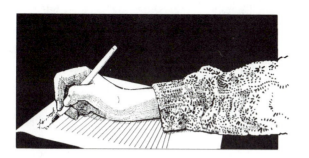

CHAPTER OBJECTIVES

1. Learn to use visuals to aid memory.
2. Recognize the value of organization to aid memory.
3. Learn notes preparation.

The temptation to rely on notes is a strong one. We've all had the experience of intending to say something that completely slips our minds as we stand in front of people. Returning to our seats will trigger several ideas we wish we had included. As one wag put it when complimented on the great presentation he had given, "You should have heard the one I gave after I sat down!"

However, we've already established in Chapter 18, "Delivery Choices," that reading a presentation is less than useful. How can we help ourselves remember everything when we're under presentation stress? Some hints will improve our use of notes.

Sometimes my notes get in my way!

PREPARE

Don't learn the tricks of the trade. Learn the trade.

– Anonymous

Nothing compensates for sloppy preparation. A presentation that is a jumble of thought and ideas is impossible to remember, no matter how hard you try. Similarly, one you just "wing" may be clever and entertaining—but will lack the substance necessary to make the presentation succeed.

> **Nothing compensates for inadequate preparation.**

ORGANIZE

Good organization is the first step to remembering (see Chapter 4, "The FourMat"). Good organization allows the mind to track from one idea to the next. Main points to be explained by supporting information allow logic and clarity to nudge your mind.

Good organization allows the mind to track from one idea to the next.

Now, in spite of every preparation and organization, you may feel you still need something to prod your fuzzy memory as you work. That is possible without using notes as an interruptive crutch. Here are some ways.

1. Use visual aids to contain your notes.

A flip chart, a chalkboard or whiteboard, or an overhead transparency can be used to keep the presentation going smoothly. Display such a visual during your introduction and refer to it during transitions from point to point. That not only helps the presenter remember where to go next but also maps the presentation beautifully for the listeners.

2. Use edges of visuals to remind you where you're going next.

The frame of an overhead can contain a key word, an example of support, or directions of what to do next. The "butterfly" wings of overhead transparencies can serve the same way.

Do not look where you fell, but where you slipped.

– African Proverb

No gain is so certain as that which proceeds from the economical use of what you already have.

– Latin Proverb

Presenters often write their notes on the edges of the transparency.

A flip chart with tiny notes written in pencil can be easily used by the presenter and will not be intrusive or distracting to the viewers.

Flip chart users often write presentation reminders with hand-written notes in the upper left-hand corner.

> # Use edges of visuals to remind you where you're going next.

3. Use paper or note cards.

If all else fails, you can return to standard paper or note cards. But don't return to standard usage of them. The following ideas may help:

Write big. In front of people, and under stress, you'll have difficulty finding your place in small writing. Don't write anything out word for word. And don't write full sentences or ideas. Write key words big with space around them.

Keep notes simple and easy to read.

Write key words big with space around them.

Don't hold notes in your hands. Having something in your hands is distracting at best and uses up your best visual aids (your hands) for something far less important. Put notes on a nearby table. You'll have plenty of time to walk over to them to refresh your memory. You have the additional advantage of moving about, which is interesting, and of allowing your mind to work without a crutch.

Do not quench your inspiration and your imagination; do not become the slave of your model.

– Vincent Van Gogh

Having something in your hands is distracting and uses up your best visual aids (your hands) for something far less important.

My key words are my visuals.

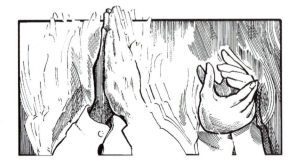

CHAPTER SUMMARY

Preparing organized material is the best way to remember under the pressure of the moment. Proper use of notes can keep presentations organized, flowing, and complete. Other memory-jarring techniques such as visuals, key words on edges of visuals, or clear and simple note cards can help polish a presentation.

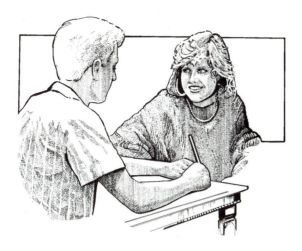

EXERCISES

1. Using the process described in this book (purpose, audience, brainstorm, organize into The FourMat), prepare a one-minute presentation on any subject. Pay attention to the organization and notice how well you remember the whole presentation when the organization is in place. Videotape the presentation.

2. Now use the same process and prepare a three-minute presentation. Do you have difficulty remembering three minutes' worth of material more than one minute's worth? Videotape the presentation.

3. Prepare a simple visual with only your three main points on it. Notice how the visual helps you keep track of your train of thought. Videotape yourself using the visual.

4. Try any of the suggestions in this chapter by putting key words on the edges of the overhead or flipchart. Notice how comfortably you can then work in front of the group. Videotape yourself practicing the technique.

5. Prepare notes on a card or a sheet of paper. Remember to keep them simple and to write them BIG. Also, remember to place them on a table or desk at the side, so your hands remain free to gesture. Videotape yourself using your notes.

CHAPTER 25 Stress Reduction

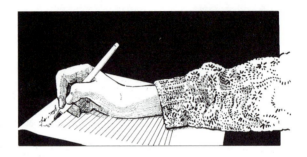

CHAPTER OBJECTIVES

1. Know the nature of stress.
2. Recognize the difference between physical and mental stress.
3. Use long-term methods to manage stress.
4. Use short-term methods to manage stress.

An experienced presenter quipped, "We no longer have the fight-or-flight syndrome; now we have 'sit and sweat'!" In saying that, he was referring to the days when stress made our central nervous systems produce adrenalin to give us power to run or courage to engage in battle. No wonder stress is so uncomfortable when we can do neither. Think about how your boss would react if, at the beginning of a presentation today, the two of you engaged in "fight or flight."

Stress is so familiar in our world today that clinics and workshops abound to help us reduce stress. Experts on meditation, time management, and psychology work in hospitals, corporations, and universities to teach us ways to manage stress. Biofeedback is available to give each of us information about our own reactions to stress. Coping skills become paramount in surviving too many things to do, too much ambition, too many bills to pay, too much pain in relationships, and too much pressure to succeed.

The modern world seems to be about human *doing,* not human *being.* Add the pressure of an important presentation to the already-stressed body and mind, and you can easily see why people fear speaking before a group more than they fear death, spiders, elevators, or snakes.

The human brain starts working the moment you are born and never stops until you stand up to speak in public.

– Sir George Jessel

> **The modern world seems to be about human *doing,* not human *being*.**

THE NATURE OF STRESS

When our well-being or safety is threatened, our bodies develop physiological ways to cope. These same physiological functions can be channeled to improve the quality of a presentation.

Stress attacks the body in two ways—physically and mentally.

Does your stress show?

Any person may exhibit many different forms of *physical stress*. The forms include rapid heart beat, sweating, clammy hands, shaky knees, quivering voice, or rapid breathing. Do you recognize any of these as your own?

Mental stress includes forgetting what you've prepared, blanking out completely, feeling confused, or experiencing fear (which, of course, manifests itself in physical ways as well).

Stress attacks the body in two ways— physically and mentally.

How can we prepare to manage such feelings? Let's consider gathering a "preparedness tool kit," somewhat like we prepare for an emergency. The first two tools we'll place in the tool kit will be one to work on long-term management of stress and one to work on short-term management of stress.

LONG-TERM STRESS-REDUCTION TOOLS

You can do what you have to do, and sometimes you can do it even better than you think you can.

– Jimmy Carter

Long-term stress can be relieved in three ways:
• Prepare.
• Practice.
• Present.

Prepare

Good preparation relieves anxiety by giving the presenter confidence in what will be covered. Using the techniques described in other areas of this book will increase the quality of preparation. Be sure to focus on the audience and the purpose. Then, carefully develop content.

Practice

Rehearsal helps. However, you can rehearse in many ways. Try some of the following ways. They are listed in order of importance as the time of presentation approaches.
• Practice in your imagination.
• Practice at your desk.

- Practice out loud.
- Practice in front of a mirror.
- Invite a trusted colleague to watch and give feedback.
- Practice using a video camera so you can critique yourself.

Present

As difficult as the process may be to you, take every opportunity to present. This kind of experience is the most important for the teaching value. The more you present, the better you will become at it. Another side benefit you will discover is that a presenter in an organization is *visible*. Visible people get promotions. Your career will be benefited when you are a good presenter. Good presenters get opportunities to grow and to develop themselves and the organization.

> **Take advantage of every opportunity to present.**

SHORT-TERM STRESS-REDUCTION TOOLS

Short-term stress can be managed both mentally and physically.

The Management of Mental Stress

Help yourself manage mental stress by doing the following:
- Focus on the message—not on yourself.
- Use visual aids to help you remember.
- Organize carefully—the clearer and simpler your organization, the easier your message is to remember.
- Give yourself positive feedback ("I can do this," "I've done it before," "I'm prepared," and "I will succeed").
- Remember the audience wants you to succeed. (You won't find many audience members who say, "I hope she fails; I hope this is a crummy presentation; I hope this is boring!")
- Imagine yourself succeeding.
- Imagine yourself relaxed.
- Take a mental vacation. In your mind, imagine yourself in your favorite vacation spot.
- Do a physical activity, *mentally*.

I can see that I will do well.

Imagine yourself succeeding!

The Management of Physical Stress

You will never be the person you can be if pressure, tension, and discipline are taken out of your life.

– James G. Bilkey

Physical stress can be approached in two ways. One is privately before the presentation begins; another is subtly just before you stand up to begin your presentation.

Privately,

- Do 10 jumping jacks. (Doing so helps expend excess energy— sort of like the "flight" we talked about. This exercise is also useful for the low-energy person who tends to get better while warming up. This exercise becomes the warm-up.)
- Stretch out.
- Walk quickly down the hall and back, or walk around the building.

Subtly, in front of people,

- Breathe deeply.
- Tense muscles; then relax.

- Do a physical activity, *mentally.* This idea of doing a physical activity, *mentally*, is very powerful. Some singers, unable to vocalize right before a performance, can actually warm up their voices by *mentally* imagining they are singing warm-up scales. Some athletes can limber up their muscles in the same way. We are not suggesting these mental activities as substitutes for the real thing. Instead, we are suggesting them as a preparation procedure when you can't do the real thing.

Do a physical activity—mentally.

A related idea of the power of our imaginations is contained in a book called *The Read-Aloud Handbook*, by Jim Trelease (John Leo, "How the Hostages Came Through," *Time*, February 9, 1981, p. 52; Gregg W. Downey, "Keough Ponders the Lessons of Captivity," *Executive Educator*, May 1981, pp. 24–29).

As the American Embassy hostages were released in Iran after their 444 days of captivity, most were amazingly mentally healthy. As they were debriefed by their State Department doctors, the hostages detailed what had saved them during that ordeal. Their conclusion— imagination.

The hostages explained they had assigned themselves "work" to do each day in their minds. One described a train trip from India to England, including seating arrangements, passenger descriptions, and dining-car menus. Another remodeled his parents' home in his mind, room by room, even choosing wallpaper and new flooring. Another constructed an elaborate computer program. And another designed a golf course.

All these activities occurred in the minds of the hostages. We are all hostages at some time in our lives—to bad marriages, doctors' offices, freeways, or illness.

Shortly after one conservative mother heard this idea about the power of our minds, she accompanied her 12-year-old son to a rock concert. He wanted to hear the group sing, and the mother didn't think he was old enough to go alone with his friends. She volunteered to go with him.

Laughter is inner jogging.

– Norman Cousins

To the mother's dismay, she found herself hostage to a rock concert! With her new appreciation of imagination, she retreated, in her mind, to her favorite vacation spot. She summed up the experience by saying, "I have never enjoyed a concert more. My son enjoyed it too."

Another example was illustrated in the 1984 Olympics in Los Angeles. Mary Lou Retton was 15 years old and the hope of the American gymnastics team. As her achievements mounted, the public became aware, for the first time really, of the valuable role of the sports psychologist. Mary Lou said she had been working with such a professional for the entire year before the Olympics.

One of Mary Lou's exercises was to visualize, just before she fell asleep, her vault event. She was taught to see herself approach, hurdle, somersault, twist, and make a perfect landing with arms raised in triumph, while waving to the crowd as she had the gold medal hung around her neck. America watched as the results of her mental preparedness really happened. Mary Lou vaulted twice; two perfect 10s resulted!

On early morning television the next day, Kathleen Sullivan interviewed Mary Lou from Los Angeles and her parents from their home in Texas. The power of learning to deal with stress was very clear as the 15-year-old girl graciously fielded questions and dealt with the media in front of the national TV audience. Her proud and happy parents showed the natural discomfort of being thrust—vaulted—into the limelight.

You can make a difference in your own reactions to stress. You have both mental and physical means at your disposal to manage the pressure of the moment. With practice, you can learn to draw on your mental and physical resources to enable you to improve your performances.

> *Cultivate ease and naturalness. Have all your powers under command. Take possession of yourself, as in this way only can you take possession of your audience. If you are ill at ease, your listeners will be also. Always speak as though there were only one person in the hall whom you had to convince. Plead with him, argue with him, arouse him, touch him, but feel that your audience is one being whose confidence and affection you want to win.*
>
> – Charles Reade

Practice will enable you to improve your performances because it will help you learn to draw on your mental and physical resources.

CHAPTER SUMMARY

Learning to manage stress is a part of the modern world. Stress manifests itself in both physical and mental ways. By dealing with both physical and mental stress in long-term and short-term ways, we can improve our quality of life as well as our presentations.

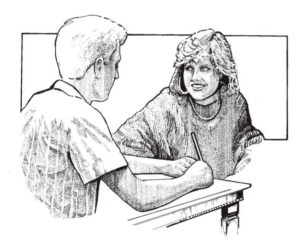

EXERCISES

1. Establish a regular physical exercise program to manage stress in the long term. At least twice a week, walk for two miles or more, jog, use an exercise bicycle, lift weights, swim, play tennis or racquetball, or ski. Do *something*.

2. Prepare a three-minute presentation to give to a group. Monitor your own stress symptoms as you prepare and as you present. Are you panicked? Sweaty? Clammy? Cold? Does your heart beat too fast? Your breathing become irregular? Your knees shake?

Make a list of your symptoms that are physical and a list of the symptoms that are mental. You may have more of one than the other. Then, make a plan of this chapter's suggestions that will help you reduce stress in the specific areas you feel it.

3. Put calming, beautiful music on your stereo system and lie down comfortably on the floor. As the music plays, allow yourself to form restful, peaceful pictures in your mind. Breathe evenly and deeply. Relax.

4. Prepare a mental movie. This movie becomes your own special retreat. The preparation requires some time at first, but later you can return to it mentally and receive the benefits rather quickly. Imagine yourself walking down a road to a place you love to go—the mountains, the beach, a meadow. (Nature seems to inspire a reduction of stress.) Now imagine every detail of the scene. How does the sky look? How does the ground feel? What things are growing there? Do creatures live there? (If they do, they are surely peaceful, friendly creatures.) See the place. Enjoy the beauty. And store the movie away to be retrieved when necessary.

5. Another kind of mental movie is one where you see yourself perform. Imagine you are sitting in a room with the very best presenter you know. As you watch this presenter, imagine you are called upon to help with the presentation at the front of the room. You willingly accept and work side by side with your favorite presenter. Eventually, you realize the presenter has taken your seat and you are left to finish the presentation alone. You realize that this is no problem, that you are prepared, and that you can see by the looks on the listeners' faces you are doing very well. As you finish, the room erupts in applause, which you accept graciously. Play this mental movie when you need it.

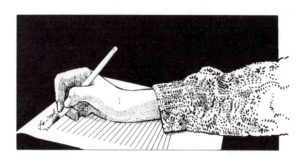

CHAPTER OBJECTIVES

1. Know how to deal with questions asked by the audience.
2. Phrase questions to encourage interaction.
3. Listen for subtext.

We want to look at questions and answers from two directions. One is how the presenter deals with questions asked by the audience; the other is how the presenter deals with questions the presenter asks—in other words, interaction.

Education is a progressive discovery of our ignorance.

– Will Durant

DEALING WITH THE AUDIENCE'S QUESTIONS

As a presenter, whether in front of a classroom, in a board room, during an interview, or in an informal gathering, you'll recognize that sinking feeling of blankness when someone asks a question to which you don't know the answer. Such an experience can make a presenter dread the very thought of completing the prepared material and opening up the time for questions.

Oh no! Someone has a question!

However, we encourage you to take heart. Questions indicate interest, and they create valuable opportunities for clarification. A few suggestions will make the whole experience positive for the presenter and listeners alike.

Questions indicate interest and create valuable opportunities for clarification.

---

1. Schedule the time for questions.

In the early stages of the presentation, say something like, "Please ask questions any time you like," or "Please hold your questions until the end of the presentation," or "I'll stop at the end of each section to ask for questions, so you may want to keep track of what questions you want to ask." Then, follow through.

2. Prepare your material thoroughly.

Have facts and figures available, even though you don't plan to use them. They may come in handy during the question-and-answer section.

3. Anticipate specific questions.

Having analyzed your audience and your purpose thoroughly, you may already know the areas the audience is likely to want to explore more thoroughly. Prepare accordingly.

4. Have a friend listen to your presentation and ask questions.

Our friends and colleagues can be objective the first time they hear the material. Take advantage of that first-time objectivity. They will come up with 90 percent of the questions your listeners will ask.

5. Prepare to be gracious and respectful.

Good manners go a long way in creating clear communication. Be gracious and respectful in answering questions, even if you are hurried or irritated.

Each of the above suggestions can be practiced and planned for when the audience asks questions. Now, what will help while you're in the question-and-answer interaction situation? The following suggestions will help you receive questions from the audience.

- Make eye contact with the questioner.
- Nod or vocalize to indicate your understanding.
- Include the whole group in the answer by making eye contact around the room. In large groups, restate the question to be sure everyone hears.
- Organize your responses. The FourMat works well here, too.
- Respond concisely.
- If you don't know the answer, say, "I don't know, but I'll find out and get back to you." Then, be sure you do.

Disdain not your inferior, though poor, since he may be your superior in wisdom, and the noble endowments of mind.

– George Shelley

And I have strong feelings about the second part of your question!

A great deal of the time, when people hear someone say something they don't immediately understand, they assume that it's false and try to imagine what could be wrong with the person saying it that would cause him or her to say anything so ridiculous.

— Suzette Haden Elgin

Occasionally, you may get into a situation where the questioners are out to make you and your ideas look foolish. We've seen such exchanges at national press conferences, at school board meetings, and even at work. You can handle such situations. This skill improves with practice. The following suggestions may help.

- Keep your cool. Here's the place your good manners and calm preparation can really defuse a situation.
- Avoid the temptation to argue, answer sarcastically, or try to make the questioner look foolish.
- Try to agree with *something* the questioner says—for example, the relevance of differing viewpoints to different audiences or the right of the questioner to express a point of view.
- Remain in control of the situation, the time, and the group. Be firm, but gentle.

A good way to keep control of the situation, the time, and the group is to return to the major points you want to emphasize. Restate them clearly and then move on to the next question or complete the session.

> **A good way to keep control of the situation, the time, and the group is to return to the major points you want to emphasize.**

ENCOURAGING INTERACTION

Now that we've considered how the presenter deals with questions from the audience, let's look at the questions the presenter asks. In other words, let's look at *interaction.*

Some situations call for insights from the audience. This interaction is the responsibility of the presenter, the leader, or the teacher. Any new presenter recognizes the feeling of asking a question of a group of blank faces and getting single-syllable responses. Focusing on the audience and the purpose, and knowing how to form questions for the desired responses, can be helpful.

Two considerations we discussed in Chapter 5, "The Purpose Statement," are (1) knowing the purpose of the presentation and (2) analyzing the audience who will hear it. These two considerations are basic to interaction. You have to know what you are trying to accomplish and who is listening.

Interaction is a valuable way to keep attention and to monitor the concerns of the audience. Use the opportunity to really *teach*. We will return to the dangers of allowing interaction in a moment.

PHRASING QUESTIONS FOR DESIRED RESPONSES

Two kinds of questions exist. We call one closed and the second open—or open ended. They elicit different responses. Careful presenters or facilitators can orchestrate discussions by carefully phrasing the questions.

Closed Questions

Closed questions require a specific answer. "When did Columbus discover America?" "What was our sales increase last year?" "Who developed our business plan?"

Closed questions are good for directing a line of thinking, for helping a reticent audience member contribute and feel successful, or for constructing a knowledge of facts. When you want interaction or discussion, avoid questions where a yes or no answer can be used.

> ## Closed questions require a specific answer.

Open Questions

On the other hand, open questions have no specific answer. "What insights do you have into our customer-relations problems?" "What changes should we make in our advertising?" "How might we afford computer training?"

Open questions are excellent for problem solving, for brainstorming, and for eliciting ideas and discussion from a group of people.

> ## Open questions have no specific answer.

FACING SMALL GROUPS VERSUS LARGE GROUPS

Some people think interaction can't take place in large groups. A skillful facilitator can work with 150–200 people and still encourage interaction. The biggest drawback to group size is the difficulty of hearing one another when sound amplification is not possible. If you can overcome that problem by using a microphone, standing to speak, or clearly repeating the comments, interaction can still be valuable.

IMPROVING INTERACTION THROUGH CAREFUL LISTENING

You can improve interaction through careful listening. In the process, you should listen for the subtext—what the audience member *means* beyond the words spoken. See Chapter 27, "Listening," for additional ideas on listening.

> **Listen for the subtext—what the audience member means beyond the words spoken.**

VALIDATING COMMENTS

An important part of encouraging interaction is validating the comments made by everyone. A nod of the head, a "thank you," or an "I never thought of it that way" all make the audience member feel the comment has been validated—and thereby encourages others to comment as well.

Successful interaction means participants feel their contributions are valid and important for the group. Again, nothing can substitute for good manners in interacting with others.

USING TRANSITION

Encouraging interaction is scary because it could make the presenter or the facilitator lose some control. We never know what someone may say or what path the comment may direct us toward. Using transitions to redirect the discussion allows the facilitator to complete the planned material. Try these ideas:

- Prepare carefully.
- Focus on a main purpose.
- Be prepared to "change horses in midstream" if the audience catches hold of an idea that needs exploration more detailed than the one you chose.
- Encourage moving on by using statements like, "Two more comments and then we'll move on" or "That idea moves us right into the next main point."
- Practice, practice, practice.

Using transitions to redirect the discussion allows the facilitator to complete the planned material.

Here is one more thought about dealing with questions and answers. Just about everyone will have a few minutes in the spotlight if only to ask or respond to a question. Such an interaction could be a media opportunity. The most common of us have been thrust into the limelight. The immediacy of media puts even the most ordinary into public situations we are not prepared for. Consider these ideas in dealing with being thrust into the spotlight of the media.

- Answer questions concisely and directly.
- Have facts, data, and figures with you to add credibility to your answers.
- Learn how to "bridge." Answer briefly, and then return to your prepared material.
- Turn a negative into a positive.
- Don't hurry. Pause for a moment to construct your answer.
- Use positive nonverbal communication (see Chapter 20, "Body Language"). Make eye contact, control hand and body movement, and smile.

Most of all, remember you are in charge of the space and the time. You can manage both by using the concepts in this book.

The last of the human freedoms—to choose one's attitude in any given set of circumstances, to choose one's own way.

– Victor Frankl

You are in charge of the space and the time.

CHAPTER SUMMARY

Dealing with questions and answers and encouraging audience inter-action are two parts of questions and answers. By preparing for questions, you can improve the quality of your presentations. Learning to use both closed questions and open questions to stimulate interaction increases the audience interest and involvement. Learning question-and-answer skills and practicing them in all kinds of situations will increase the presenter's abilities to deal with them.

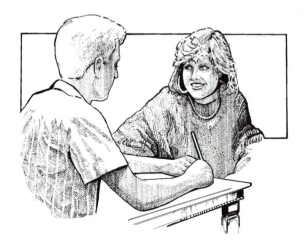

EXERCISES

1. As you prepare your presentation, prepare a list of possible questions that may arise. Have someone else listen to you rehearse and supply questions as well. Now, prepare answers to those questions. Remember to organize the answers. (This is also a

good way to adjust your content to include the best possible information.)

2. Listen to question-and-answer radio and television programs such as *Face the Nation, Meet the Press, Larry King Live,* and others. Any news conference will also be useful. Focus on how questions are answered effectively. Listen for organization and bridges, returning to very important points. Imagine words you might have used to answer. (This exercise is also useful in a group.) Write a one-page response to what you hear.

3. Play 20 Questions. One person thinks of something, and another person is allowed 20 questions to discover what the first person is thinking of. Use "closed" questions—those that can be answered with only a yes or a no.

4. In preparing a group project, assign one group member to "What if ..." every situation. Such exploration can improve presenters' skills in dealing with questions and answers.

CHAPTER 27 Listening

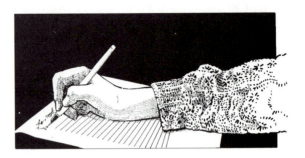

CHAPTER OBJECTIVES

1. Understand the difference between hearing and listening.
2. Use interaction to clarify listening.
3. Learn to understand the speaker of English as a second language.

We spend as much as 80 percent of our waking time communicating in one form or another. Conservative estimates indicate that 50 percent of that communicating time is spent in listening. Those facts present us with an interesting dilemma. The dilemma is that we need to spend as much time learning how to listen as we do learning how to speak. Few of us have had any formal training in the very skill that takes up half our waking lives.

Listening is a skill. The listening expertise we possess we have developed through day-to-day experiences with family and friends. Even though we have spent years of formal schooling on other communication skills—reading, writing, and, yes, even speaking—we don't enroll for Listening 101. We should.

Listening is a skill.

Scholars are preparing ways to understand and teach the importance of listening. Today, organizations such as the International Listening Association have been formed to improve listening skills in colleges and universities. Organizations develop tests, teaching units, and chapters in books like this one. Still, Listening 101 is not in most curricula.

Researchers conducted one study at different levels of school. In the first grade, the class was interrupted and was asked what the teacher just said. Ninety percent of the students knew. (If you've ever known first graders well, you know they can repeat everything that happened at school from the time they arrived.) The same interruptions occurred in other classes. In the second grade, 80 percent knew; in junior high, 44 percent knew; and in high school, 28 percent knew.

In a study of college freshmen, students retained only 50 percent of a 10-minute lecture and lost half of this material in 48 hours. What happens as we go along to make us listen less?

Perhaps we can improve this self-taught skill by raising our consciousness.

But this joyful, imaginative, impassioned energy dies out of us very young. Why?... Because we don't respect it in ourselves and keep it alive by using it. And because we don't keep it alive in others by listening to them.

– Brenda Ueland

**We spend as much as 80 percent of our waking
time communicating in one form or another.**

UNDERSTANDING THE DIFFERENCE BETWEEN HEARING AND LISTENING

Listener: A person who "is not only popular everywhere, but after awhile he knows something."

– Wilson Mizner

Hearing is the physical phenomenon of sound being received through the ears. Listening encompasses much more than receiving sound. Listening even suggests using eyes, experience, understanding, and body language, as well as ears. Listening means activity, not passive receiving. Listening takes energy and attention.

> **Listening encompasses much more than receiving sound. Listening takes energy and attention.**

It pays to listen.

LEARNING TO FOCUS ON THE SPEAKER

Jean Jenkins, in *Voice, Diction, and Interpretation,* suggests five levels of listening. She suggests that each level requires more listening skill development than the preceding level. The levels include listening for the following reasons:

1. Entertainment.
2. Escape.
3. Inspiration.
4. Information gathering and ideas.
5. Evaluation and opinions.

We think her list is an effective one. Recognizing that different levels of work are required at different levels of listening simplifies the effort, but still doesn't teach how to develop the skill. The following list suggests ways to improve listening at different levels.

1. Develop an attitude of wanting to listen.
2. Stop talking.
3. Increase your vocabulary.
4. Get rid of interruptions.
5. Find something to agree with.
6. Watch the speaker.
7. Take notes.
8. Organize.
9. Anticipate.
10. Outline.
11. Apply the speaker's ideas to your own life, thoughts, and interests.
12. Ignore "red-flag" words.
13. Get the main idea.
14. Listen for what is not said.
15. Concentrate on the message, not the delivery.
16. Try to hear the speaker's point of view.
17. Withhold evaluation until comprehension is complete.

Develop an attitude of wanting to listen.

However, listening improvement still eludes us unless we first discover for ourselves and admit that our own listening is weak. How can we come to this realization?

Listening is a magnetic and strange thing, a creative force. The friends who listen to us are the ones we move toward, and we want to sit in their radius. When we are listened to, it creates us, makes us unfold and expand.

– Karl Menninger

USING INTERACTION TO UNDERSTAND

It is the province of knowledge to speak and it is the privilege of wisdom to listen.

– Oliver Wendell Holmes

In small group presentation situations—unlike large group lectures—the presenter has the advantage of being able to discover how much the listeners understand. Question-and-answer sessions are common, either during the presentation, or scheduled at the end of it. Good presenters train themselves to welcome interaction with the audience. Such interaction lets presenters know how the message is being received. Immediate adjustments can be made to help further understanding. (See Chapter 26, "Questions and Answers.")

> **Good presenters train themselves to welcome interaction with the audience.**

DISCOVERING THE UNDERLYING MESSAGE

Here is the ultimate goal of listening. A good listener answers this question: What does the speaker *mean*? To know the speaker's meaning is a skill every listener should seek. Such a skill would be the true gift of communication.

No longer would we be bound by the words exchanged, but we would use all the cues—body language, voice, intent, feelings, interest, respect, and the words—to exchange meanings. True communication means understanding.

> **True communication means understanding.**

UNDERSTANDING THE ESL SPEAKER

In this global, international, ever-smaller world we live in, we are privileged to meet and communicate with interesting people from many interesting places. Many of them speak English as a second language (ESL). Many of them speak beautifully, but often the framework of another language overpowers English pronunciation and syntax—and we find it difficult to be sure we understand.

The following behaviors may help you understand the ESL speaker:

- Exhibit a warm, friendly smile.
- Use attentive body language to indicate active listening.
- Pursue a questioning attitude for clarification.
- Repeat what you thought you heard: "Do you mean…?"
- Build trust in a long-term relationship so at some point you can suggest a more correct pronunciation when the listener is teachable.
- Encourage participation.
- Ask questions about interesting experiences so, as the person speaks, you can begin to familiarize yourself with pronunciation.

In Chapter 19, "Congruence," we talked about integrity. We return to it here. Listening requires an integrity and sincerity of purpose that allows you to focus on the value and worth of what another is saying—even if you disagree.

> **Listening requires the integrity and sincerity of purpose that allows you to focus on the value and worth of what another is saying— even if you disagree.**

CHAPTER SUMMARY

Listening occupies a major portion of our communication time; yet we usually learn it by chance. Some effort must be made to become better listeners. By focusing on developing our listening skills, we can improve our interaction during presentations and understanding of others' communication.

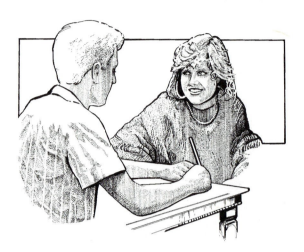

EXERCISES

1. During a presentation, a speech, or a lecture, imagine you are responsible for writing an executive summary for the boss. Take brief notes to create an outline you will flesh out later. Write the executive summary from the outline.

2. Play a variation of the children's game known as Telegraph. Have three or four people leave the room. Explain an assignment or a project that might have to be completed on the job and have that person explain it to the next, and that person to the next, and so on. Observe how difficult the process of retaining the clarity of the assignment is when the assignment must pass through several listeners.

3. Two people can demonstrate how communication can increase by allowing the listener to ask questions. Supply the speaker with a sheet of paper on which several shapes are drawn. Then, on the chalkboard or on paper, the listener draws what the speaker directs. The first time don't let the listener ask any questions. The second time, when the listener is allowed to ask questions, the correctness of the drawing will increase.

4. After a serious conversation with a friend, write down what you understood the friend to say. Don't focus on words; focus on meaning. Check with your friend to assess the correctness of your notes.

Sensitivity Considerations CHAPTER 28

CHAPTER OBJECTIVES

1. Become aware of audience concerns.
2. Recognize sexist language.
3. Expect the unexpected.

Some people seem to be born with a sensitivity to others. Such people seem aware of others' feelings and responses to what is happening. Other people seem to be born without a clue that a world of communication is going on around them. Such people do not seem to be aware of the needs of others.

> **Some people seem to be born with a sensitivity to others.**

In any case, we can learn to improve our sensitivity. By becoming aware—by having our consciousness raised—we can process immediate feedback and improve presentations and the audience's acceptance of our presentation. This awareness will increase our sensitivity.

Three directives for improving sensitivity spring to mind. They deal with avoiding sexist language, giving immediate audience feedback, and coping with the unexpected.

Be careful of how you live, you may be the only Bible some person ever reads.

– William J. Toms

AVOID SEXIST LANGUAGE

So much has been explored and talked about regarding sexist language that we may have a feeling of redundancy in reading about it again. Is it possible that presenters have "turned the corner" and reached the point where they absolutely avoid sexist language? Probably not.

We still hear groups who groan with dismay when told they must avoid any possibility of sexist language in their presentations. Apparently, some individuals still regard the directive to avoid sexist language as being unimportant. Nothing could be further from the truth.

Honey, some of my best friends are women supervisors.

Sexist language can be limiting and can easily offend an audience. One consultant had such an experience while *teaching* about sexist language. A participant raised her hand to ask why the consultant always referred to the principal in a school as a "he." Even though the consultant's own experience had been that all principals in her schools were male, she knew that was not always the case. The listener was right to raise the issue.

A primary dimension of sensitivity during presentations is to avoid sexist language. The following suggestions are suitable ways of doing so:

1. Use an appropriate alternative to the singular, masculine pronouns *he, him,* and *his* through one or more of the following procedures:

   - Eliminate the singular, masculine pronouns.
     Say,
     The student must read the text and get help from the teacher
     rather than,
     The student must read his text and get help from his teacher.
   - Use a plural pronoun.
     Say,
     When workers request vacation time, they must use Form 235
     rather than,
     When a worker requests vacation time, he must use Form 235.
   - Use genderless words.
     Say,
     You will not receive all the benefits to which you are entitled if you do not plan for them
     rather than,
     The employee will not receive all the benefits to which he is entitled if he does not plan for them.
   - Use job titles or functions.
     Say,
     The supervisor must permit a break every morning
     rather than,
     He must permit a break every morning.

Years ago I preferred clever people...My preferred person today is one who is always aware of the needs of others, or their pain and fear and unhappiness, and their search for self-respect...I once liked clever people. Now I like good people.

– Solomon Bennett Freehof

- Change the pronoun to an article.
  Say,
  When an employee uses a personal computer at home...
  rather than,
  *When an employee uses his personal computer
  at home...*
- Use the passive voice.
  Say,
  *The workers should be given a break at 10 AM by the
  supervisor*
  rather than,
  The supervisor should give his workers a break at 10 AM.
- Use the person's name.
  Say,
  *When Mr. Martin, the supervisor, arrives, he will open the
  cash registers*
  rather than,
  *When the supervisor arrives, he will open the cash
  registers.*
- Repeat the noun.
  Say,
  *If the supervisor cannot attend the meeting, the supervisor
  must send a replacement*
  rather than,
  *If the supervisor cannot attend the meeting, he must send a
  replacement.*
- Include the feminine pronoun.
  Say,
  *If the supervisor cannot attend, he or she must send a
  replacement*
  rather than,
  *If the supervisor cannot attend, he must send a
  replacement.*

2. Use an appropriate alternative to the generic use of the word
   man. Use such words as *person, human, individual, people,* and
   men and women.
3. Use appropriate substitutions for *man* suffixes and prefixes. Use
   such words as *businessperson, executive, leader, chair, presiding
   officer, salesperson* and *representative*.

4. Use appropriate substitutions for occupational titles containing the suffix *man*. Use such titles as *delivery clerk, supervisor, repairer, salesperson, sales representative*, and *sales agent*.

5. Avoid sex-role stereotyping in words and phrases. Avoid such expressions as *woman driver, weak sister, man-sized job, female doctor, male nurse, coed, secretary…she, executive…he, the girls*, and *the females*.

INTERPRET IMMEDIATE AUDIENCE FEEDBACK

Another useful way to be sensitive is to monitor audience feedback even as you present. At first, this process can seem rather like patting your head and rubbing your stomach at the same time.

But, with practice, you can process the information the audience is giving you at the same time you speak. How can you do so? Watch for eye contact—are members of the audience listening to you? How are postures? Are members of the audience slumped in chairs? Is the audience alert?

Are side conversations occurring so participants lose contact with you? If so, are the conversations about the subject you are working on? That is a sure indication you need to explore something in more depth.

Are the participants talking about something else? That is a sure indication you are boring the group and need to move on.

I'd rather be surfing

Monitor audience feedback as you present.

Are the participants restless? Do they need a break? Or does riveted silence indicate they are hanging on to your every word?

Pay attention. A little practice can give you a world of information. A good way to practice is to watch the audience feedback while someone else presents. Then, you have to concentrate on only one thing at a time and can hone your skills.

Discretion of speech is more than eloquence, and to speak agreeably to him with whom we deal is more than to speak in good words or in good order.

– Sir Francis Bacon

COPE WITH THE UNEXPECTED

One student's first experience with the unexpected was when she was a college student. One midday in November, she and her classmates heard that President Kennedy had been shot. Almost nothing else mattered for several days as members of the class listened intently to every news report and to every explanation—trying to understand something that was totally foreign to them.

The student was amazed that school activities—the upcoming examination, the due dates for papers, and the plans for the weekend—all became insignificant as the students focused on something much larger.

One consultant for Exxon flew into Newark, New Jersey, on a Sunday night and prepared to meet participants the next morning. Exxon was bringing in managers from various areas of the United States to do some training. Already in the hotel were three participants from Texas who watched in horror on television as a hurricane swept through their neighborhoods. With telephone lines down, they could not reach their families to find out how their lives had been affected.

Tact is the knack of making a point without making an enemy.

– Howard W. Newton

The next three days of the workshop were vastly different from normal as the group worked, waited, and watched for news about the families of those three participants. Members of the group didn't stop work; they just tried to help. They returned to the subject often, watched different channels on television to get the most coverage, and cheered when the successful phone calls finally confirmed that all three families were unharmed by the storm. Sensitivity matters.

Interestingly, that same week the World Series in San Francisco was interrupted by an earthquake. The same group's attention was riveted again on those events. All members of the group knew somebody in San Francisco, and the reports of collapsed freeways and broken bridges affected everyone. The feeling of sensitivity was pervasive among members of the group.

In dealing with sensitivity, perhaps we can't find a way to explain how to handle every situation. However, by being aware of the needs of the group, watching for an individual's concerns, and constructing our presentations so we bring the group together rather than drive the group members apart by insensitivity, we will improve our presentations.

The words of some men are thrown forcibly against you and adhere like burrs.

– Henry David Thoreau

Construct your presentations so you bring members of the group together rather than drive them apart.

CHAPTER SUMMARY

Sensitivity to others is a positive communication tool. By avoiding sexist language and other offensive references, we can develop trust between presenters and listeners. Listeners in the audience provide feedback even while the presenter is at work. Sensitive presenters learn to monitor feedback and adjust a presentation to keep an audience involved.

Mend your speech a little, lest it mar your fortunes.

– King Lear

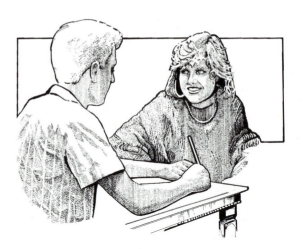

EXERCISES

Preparing exercises for this chapter is extremely difficult. How do you prepare for an emergency? Firefighters, for example, do so by simulating the emergency. In this chapter, because presenters are not dealing with the emergency itself—the hurricane, the earthquake—but dealing with an audience concerned about the event, simulating the emergency seems impractical. However, perhaps the following will help:

1. Conduct a group discussion about how group members dealt with public situations after emergencies. The disasters could be large-scale ones like flood or fire; the disasters could be personal ones like a death in the family or loss of a job.

2. Read books on man/woman communication like Deborah Tannen's *You Just Don't Understand* or Suzette Haden Elgin's *Genderspeak.*

3. Prepare and videotape a five-minute presentation on one concept or chapter from either of the books mentioned in Exercise 2.

4. Prepare and videotape a five-minute presentation on a way you might encourage colleagues or classmates to be more sensitive to others' needs.

5. Conduct a group discussion about how to increase sensitivity during a business presentation.

The Role of Silence CHAPTER 29

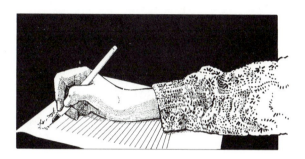

CHAPTER OBJECTIVES

1. Recognize the power of silence.
2. Use silence as a tool.
3. Understand silence as emphasis.

A powerful technique in a presentation is not speaking at all. Silence can be used to enhance the quality of the presentation and, most especially, to point out or emphasize and give meaning to words.

> ## Silence can be used to enhance the quality of the presentation.

However, the typical presenter is leery of silence. Surely, presenters think listeners assume silence means lack of preparation, a blank mind, little knowledge—something negative by any standard.

Strangely, being in front of others causes us to reduce our ability to estimate time. As a result, the silence we undergo feels like eons to the presenter—but actually is only a few seconds to the audience. Silence proves useful and provides time to absorb, process, formulate questions, and understand. Silence, properly used, becomes an instrument in the orchestra, playing a skillful solo part.

> **Silence proves useful and provides time to absorb, process, formulate questions, and understand.**

USING THE PAUSE

[Macaulay] has occasional flashes of silence that make his conversation perfectly delightful.

– Sydney Smith

The word that follows a pause takes on added meaning. For example, notice the difference in meaning in the following sentence—depending on where the pause is placed.

The international spy in the red hat is missing.

The / international spy in the red hat is missing.

The international / spy in the red hat is missing.

The international spy / in the red hat is missing.

The international spy in / the red hat is missing.

The international spy in the / red hat is missing.

The international spy in the red / hat is missing.

The international spy in the red hat / is missing.

The international spy in the red hat is / missing.

When so much is riding on silence, no wonder we attempt to fill every break in our stream of words with *uh* or *um,* those wretched nonwords that intrude into otherwise interesting information.

When you have nothing to say, say nothing.

– Charles Caleb Colton

DEVELOPING UNDERSTANDING OF EMPHASIS TECHNIQUES

Silence is only one emphasis technique. Other techniques help the skillful presenter direct the attention and understanding of the listeners to the most important information.

Imagine that we carry a tool kit of emphasis techniques. We will place in it tools that will come in handy. With our tool of silence, we include the tool of voice variation, the tool of gesturing, and the tool of using the space in the room. In addition, we should include the tool of using visual aids, one of telling stories, and one of using eye contact.

What is the meaning of having a suitable tool kit? It means that an "attention getter" at the beginning of a presentation is not enough. It means the presenter must do something to get attention again and again. Here's where the tool kit becomes useful. Use a voice variety here, a visual aid there, and silence here. Soon, a presentation has been greatly improved. Additional emphasis information can be found in Chapter 10, "Access."

The presenter must do something to get attention again and again.

ENHANCING CLARITY AND PURPOSE THROUGH THE USE OF SILENCE

As emphasis techniques improve interest in a presentation, so do they improve our understanding of the clarity and purpose in a presentation. Silence should be full of purpose. For example, silence is not just lack of sound. Such silence directs, points out, improves, explains, and clarifies.

Blessed is the man who, having nothing to say, abstains from giving us wordy evidence of the fact.

– George Eliot

Silence is not just lack of sound.

Teaching how to use such silence is a bit difficult. However, careful observation can teach us. Watch the evening news. National newscasters have a natural and useful grasp of the effect of silence. Then, watch speakers like President Bill Clinton, Ronald Reagan, Leo Bataglia, or others; and pay attention to how good speakers use the

Before using a fine word, make a place for it!

– Joseph Joubert

pause. Then, try the silence technique yourself on videotape and critique your results. The skill of silence will develop.

"And right at that moment..."

The role of silence is a little explored but highly useful tool.

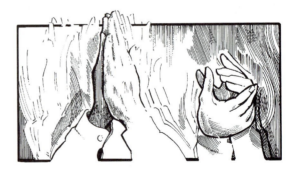

CHAPTER SUMMARY

Silence is a useful tool for the presenter. Silence is not just lack of sound and is important for listeners to use in developing understanding. When properly employed, silence becomes a powerful tool for improving understanding in communication.

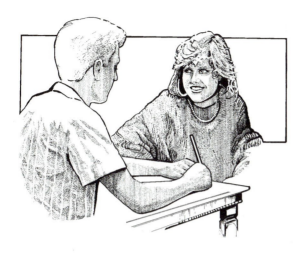

EXERCISES

1. Read aloud "How Do I Love Thee?" by Elizabeth Barrett
    Browning while placing the silence, or pauses, in different
    places. Notice the differences in meaning.

    > *How do I love thee? Let me count the ways.*
    > *I love thee to the depth and breadth and height*
    > *My soul can reach, when feeling out of sight*
    > *For the ends of Being and ideal Grace.*
    > *I love thee to the level of every day's*
    > *Most quiet need, by sun and candlelight.*
    > *I love thee freely, as men strive for Right;*
    > *I love thee purely, as men turn from Praise.*
    > *I love thee with the passion put to use*
    > *In my old griefs, and with my childhood's faith.*
    > *I love thee with a love I seemed to lose*
    > *With my lost saints—I love thee with the breath,*
    > *Smiles, tears, of all my life!—and, if God choose,*
    > *I shall but love thee better after death.*

2. To eliminate filler words like *um*, and *okay*, enlist the help of a
    colleague as you present. If the presentation is a real one, have
    the colleague count the filler words or raise a finger when you
    use one. If the presentation is in a practice situation, have the

colleague tap on a glass with a pencil or count out loud when you use a filler word. Hearing that you are using filler words seems to draw attention to them quickly and helps you to reduce them.

3. Videotape a conversation with friends and then listen to your own use of words. Chances are you use filler words all the time. In a casual situation, you can easily hear them. Once you hear them, you can begin to omit them.

4. Videotape a presentation you give and evaluate your own overuse of filler words.

PART IV
Cleaning Up
Loose Ends

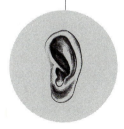

CHAPTER 30 Following Up

CHAPTER OBJECTIVES

1. To learn to pay attention to details after the presentation.
2. To understand the rationale for thank-you messages.
3. To appreciate the importance of reliability and commitment to oneself.

Several details should be attended to after the presentation to ensure effectiveness and action. Such attention helps smooth the way for final success and helps initiate opportunities to present again. Consider the following important areas.

KEEPING TRACK OF ACTION ITEMS

Most meetings and many presentations include assignments or "actions" that need to be completed. Tracking and completing action items are part of the communication function.

Find a method for keeping track of action items that fits with your own management style. The following ways have all proven successful for various professionals:

- Use a daily planner. Tracking from daily task lists and daily planning exercises helps action items remain at the front of our minds. By prioritizing tasks into A, B, and C items, many people find they deal with the most important things first.
- Use the minutes of the meeting as a reminder. Many people who keep minutes list "action" items in a separate section of the report. Action-doers can easily reference what they are responsible for.
- Use a Gantt chart. By preparing time lines and deadlines for various tasks, many professionals find the job of managing tasks to be easy.
- Use a project management chart. Both long- and short-term projects can benefit from planning how much time is required to complete portions of the tasks.

Always have some project under way… an ongoing project that goes over from day to day and thus makes each day a small unit of time.

– Dr. Lillian Troll

Find a way to track action items.

PREPARING EXIT REPORTS

The communication task required when an employee leaves a job can be beneficial to both the employee and the employer. Some companies require oral interviews; others request written reports; and some require both. We suggest that careful organization, use of The FourMat, and planned support can clarify and improve the exit report. Try it.

PREPARING THANK-YOU MESSAGES

You will never "find" time for anything. If you want time you must take it.

– Charles Buxton

Perhaps the most neglected communication task in this information age—and a very important task—is the written thank-you note, memo, or letter. Verbal expressions of thanks are enhanced by the written document that can be attached to a file.

The doggone paperwork is important!

The reward of one duty is the power to fulfill another.

– George Eliot

One recruiter refused to consider any job applicant who didn't write a thank-you letter—no matter how impressed the interviewer had been in the interview. Studies prove that employee performance improves when the boss praises the completion of an important project and writes a brief memo of thanks. An attitude of gratitude smooths rough places in many an organization.

Expressing thanks either verbally or in writing shouldn't take much time or effort. But it should occur. Make a quick phone call, or leave a phone-mail message. Have card-sized notes printed with the company logo, or run off half sheets of paper from the computer with your name at the top. But do *something* to make it easy to say "Thank you."

Of course, we recommend The FourMat organization to help you quickly dash off a note or make a phone call. The FourMat works here, too.

REACTING TO DETAIL NEEDS

From time to time, even the most practiced presenters overlook details that make it difficult to present smoothly. In addition, Murphy's law is alive and well in any presentation situation. Be assured that plenty of things can go wrong. However, quick mental (or paper) checklists can aid the presenter.

REFLECTING RELIABILITY

Years ago, while teaching in an MBA program, one professor watched a young man she really admired. The student worked hard and could be counted on to be prepared for class and to contribute to every assignment he was given.

A man is the sum of his actions, of what he has done, of what he can do. Nothing else.

– Andre Malraux

Near the end of the student's program, the professor happened to discover the student's entrance scores from two years earlier. The scores were far below those of the student's colleagues. In fact, the scores were so low that the professor couldn't understand why the student had been admitted in the first place.

At that point, the professor reflected on which of all the students in the class she would hire if she were in charge of hiring for a company. The answer came without equivocation—she would hire the young man—hands down.

When the student finished his program, he was hired right away and proved to be an excellent, qualified employee. He had one trait that outshone all the others. He was reliable.

The mode by which the inevitable comes to pass is effort.

– Oliver Wendell Holmes

The same principle is taught by Old Faithful in Yellowstone Park. Yellowstone has other more spectacular geysers, but people flock to see Old Faithful—the geyser that erupts at designated times throughout every day. Old Faithful is the geyser people can count on.

The best presenters can be counted on to prepare properly. They can be counted on to have securely supported facts and arguments. They can be counted on to *care* about the subject and the audience. They can be counted on to present *clearly*.

KEEPING COMMITMENTS

Perfect freedom is reserved for the man who lives by his own work, and in that work does what he wants to do.

– R.G. Collingwood

Another by-product of the information age is that our busy lives expand beyond the time we have to pay attention to details. Time-management seminars abound with ways to keep track of details.

However, time management has given the illusion that we can accomplish *anything*—a pressure we are having more and more trouble keeping up with. Time-management tools do enable us to keep track of dates, times, and places. Knowing such information once, instead of having to ask again when the time gets near, has helped.

Time-management tools also provide a way to track a list for which we're responsible. However, the tools must be *used*—not just owned.

Keeping commitments is what reliability is all about.

The sacrifices of the fathers are enjoyed by the children, commemorated by their grandchildren, and forgotten by their great–grandchildren.

– F. Emmett Johnson

CHAPTER SUMMARY

Only the educated are free.

– Epictetus

The end of a presentation is not necessarily the end of a project. The professional presenter completes a task by following action items, preparing exit reports, remembering to say thank you, and maintaining reliability. Attention to follow-up details improves the presentation.

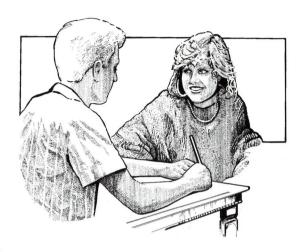

EXERCISES

1. Interview a presenter. Ask the following questions:
    a. What are some situations you have found where you
        have had to follow up with activities after a presentation?
    b. What are some specific activities?

2. Listen to a presentation. Make a list of follow-up activities the
    presenter should pursue.

3. Write a thank-you note, letter, or memo after an interview, after
    hearing a good presentation, or after giving a presentation.

4. Create a deadline chart for a presentation you must give at some
    point in the future.

CHAPTER 31 Coping

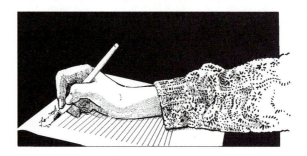

CHAPTER OBJECTIVES

1. To learn specific coping skills surrounding physical arrangements for presentation situations.
2. To learn how to cope with unfamiliar and international presentation situations.
3. To learn how to cope with jet lag and time change.
4. To learn how to stay comfortably and safely in domestic and international hotels.

Presenting is an exciting event that provides a variety of experiences. Some of the excitement comes from the variations surrounding presentations. Sometimes, the very nature of the variations causes near-catastrophic situations. The frequent presenter knows how difficult the process of being successful in every presentation is.

I thought this would work.

Far more presenters succeed than fail. Successful presenters cope rather well as situations change. The key to successful presenting in multiple settings is to expect the unexpected. As a presenter, you should prepare for less-than-perfect conditions when you present and hope the unexpected doesn't happen.

Successful presenters cope with difficult situations if they consistently achieve successful presentations. *To cope* seems to be the phrase of the day in the information age. Coping, obviously, means dealing successfully with problems; so a presenter who copes well deals successfully with unexpected situations.

Coping well is a combination of maintaining a positive attitude, preparing for the unexpected, and presenting successfully in less-than-perfect situations. This chapter deals with areas of coping by describing the general situation, offering suggestions for coping with that situation, and alluding to incidents in which presenters have successfully coped with similar situations.

When things go wrong, don't go wrong with them.

You should prepare for less-than-perfect conditions.

The five areas discussed in this chapter are the following:
- Coping as a presentation skill.
- Presenting in an international environment.
- Working with other languages.
- Coping with jet lag and time changes.
- Staying comfortably and safely in domestic and international hotels.

COPING AS A PRESENTATION SKILL

It is our duty to make the best of our misfortunes, and not to suffer passion to interfere with our interest and the public good.

– George Washington

"I can do anything" is a desirable coping attitude—a statement presenters ought to print in very large letters and place on office walls. Once you believe the "I-can-do-anything" philosophy, you *can* do almost anything; and you can usually cope successfully. Sometimes, presentation situations go so awry that the only hope you have for success is those four words.

> **Once you believe the "I-can-do-anything" philosophy, you *can* do almost anything.**

All life is an experiment, the more experiments you make the better.

– Ralph Waldo Emerson

One important presentation was made to a group of business decision-makers after an emergency evacuation of the executive suite of the building forced the presentation into the cafeteria next to a major freeway.

The presentation was rescheduled in one end of the cafeteria, and metal chairs were placed in a semicircle. An overhead projector was brought in, but a dark yellow wall had to serve as a screen. While the presentation was in session, the other end of the cafeteria was being used for food service to other employees. A hole in the wall gave a clear view of the busy freeway next to the building.

The presenter was told to ignore the distractions and begin. He began with a loud, clear voice. Only the very important information was given. The time was about one-half the planned amount. The presentation went very well.

This situation was no time for excuses and weak presentations. It was the time to get on with the presentation with the support of an "I-can-do-anything" attitude.

> ## Excuses are not a part of the successful presenter's work.

The following suggestions will help you to adapt and to cope with presentations whether at home or on the road:

1. Take care of details so the amount of adapting and coping is held to a minimum. Make sure all the arrangements have been made, including arrangements for:
   - Airline reservations.
   - Housing accommodations.
   - Directions to facilities.
   - Projectors and screens.
   - Presentation room.
   - Materials for the presentation.
   - Special instructions to everyone concerned.

> ## The best way to adapt and to cope is to solve the problem before it happens.

2. Arrive early to check out last-minute preparations. If substandard situations exist, you will then have time to cope. Suggestions for what you do after you arrive early are:
   - Visit the presentation room when appropriate.
   - Contact the audiovisual person (if possible).
   - Review all instructions with appropriate personnel.
   - Check for arrival and condition of shipped boxes.
   - Check miscellaneous rooms and presentation details.
   - Get a good night's sleep.
3. Hand carry presentation materials (visuals, tapes, slides) and a copy of all shipped materials, where possible. If materials are lost or damaged and if you have time, you can make arrangements for replacement materials. Suggestions for getting materials to the presentation site are:
   - Visually check shipped boxes and materials upon your arrival.

Communication. It is not only the essence of being human, but also a vital property of life.

– John A. Pierce

A strong positive mental attitude will create more miracles than any wonder drug.

– Patricia Neal

- Identify damaged materials.
- Determine the viability of replacing damaged materials.
- Determine the viability of on-site paper copying.
- Negotiate reproducing costs for handouts and manuals.
- Perform quality checks on reproduced material.

Presentations go well when you know you're ready.

Life is a struggle, but not a warfare.

— John Burroughs

4. Dress in travel clothes you can wear to a presentation. Also, carry with you a travel bag with a change of clothes.
   You can travel in casual business clothes if presentation clothes are carried with you on the airplane.

   Carry an extra shirt or blouse, even for a one-day trip, in case of spills or rips.

5. Stay positive while you are working through less-than-desirable situations. Complaining and expressing anger only make bad situations worse. When the people around you feel your negative vibrations, they often become difficult to work with. They are also less inclined to help you solve your problem. You have much more to lose than they do if things don't get fixed.

You can be positive as easily as you can be angry and negative.

6. Solve the most important problems first.
7. Communicate the adjustments you want made firmly and precisely
8. Work with others who are making adjustments for your presentation. Remember, they are interested in making things work for you.

Solve the most important problems first.

One presenter traveled on Sunday to make an important, one-day presentation to a major bank in New York City the next day. He traveled in jeans, a T-shirt, and white sneakers. He packed the rest of his clothes and checked them. The luggage did not arrive. The presentation began at 7:30 am.

He began in his jeans, T-shirt, and sneakers. He briefly mentioned his plight at the beginning of the meeting and then presented well. In the meantime, support staff of the bank went to a clothing store and bought a pair of slacks, a white dress shirt, a tie, and shoes. They used his credit card and paid very high prices for his one-day wardrobe. The clothes were ready at the first break.

He received an ovation when he appeared after the break in a shirt and tie. From that moment on, he never traveled in a T-shirt and jeans; and he always carried his presentation clothes with him on the airplane. He found his luggage at the airport on his way home.

Another presenter traveled to make a three-hour presentation in a distant city. She used many handouts for a presentation she had given many times. She always sent her handouts ahead of time, and she always checked to see that her materials had arrived. She made her usual check at the front desk of the hotel and found that her boxes had arrived and would be delivered to the presentation room.

As she got to the presentation room 30 minutes before her presentation, she could not find her box of materials—even though the desk clerk had assured her that her materials had arrived. She asked to see the hotel manager—only to find that the box truly was missing. She did not have a copy of her handouts.

She talked her way through the presentation with significant loss in effectiveness.

Bad times have a scientific value. These are occasions a good learner would not miss.

– Ralph Waldo Emerson

She did not complain to the audience. But thereafter, she carried a master copy of her handouts so they could be copied in an emergency.

PRESENTING IN AN INTERNATIONAL ENVIRONMENT

Many presenters are now presenting internationally. The challenges are great, but so are the rewards. Following are suggestions for presenters who work in the international arena:

He is blessed over all mortals who loses no moment of the passing life in remembering the past.

– Henry David Thoreau

1. Learn as much as you can about the culture. Speaking with someone who has presented in a particular country is a very good resource. Sometimes, you can learn more from a colleague of your nationality who has presented in that country than you can from a native of that country.

> **People appreciate travelers who know something about their country.**

2. Study the geography of the area you will visit before you arrive, so you can speak intelligently about the area. Natives of the country you visit are usually impressed when you know something about their environment.

3. Work first and play later. Many presenters take spouses or friends with them on international trips so they can do some vacationing along the way. Plan your vacation to come after you have presented so you can be "up" for the presentation and then relax afterward.

It behooves every man to remember that the work of the critic…is of altogether secondary importance, and that, in the end, progress is accomplished by the man who does…things.

– Theodore Roosevelt

> **Playing takes energy and attention, even if you are doing nothing. Your work will usually be more focused if you do it first and play later.**

4. Thoroughly check your presentation facility and equipment. Some international equipment is not compatible with the equipment you work with. Arrive a day or two early, where possible, to check everything and to rehearse your presentation under conditions of your new surroundings.

5. Ask for a contact person who speaks your language as well as the language of the visited country. Make several contacts with that person before you arrive. Then, make an immediate contact upon arrival.

6. Pay attention to food and sleep needs as you travel. Heed all the warnings about the food you eat and the water you drink if you think they may not be healthy for you. Get all the immunizations you need, and pay attention to the warnings you receive about personal health. Poor health that could be avoided during your international presentation experience is a foolish waste.

> ## Pay attention to food and sleep needs as you travel.

One presenter planned a 10-day vacation as part of an international presentation. He took his wife and teen-age daughter. The wife and daughter played and traveled while the presenter worked with the client.

The presenter felt a lot of pressure to spend time with his family, but the professional situation required more than his full-time energies. Nerves were frazzled by the time the work was completed, because neither the work nor the family got the attention they deserved.

A solution to such situations is to arrange to have the family arrive at or near the end of the professional time. The presenter can then pay adequate attention to both parties.

Another presenter prepared a presentation using substantial videotape segments. The segments were professionally prepared and would have added greatly to the presentation. She didn't check the visuals until shortly before the presentation. Then, she found that the VHS videos made in America were not compatible with the video

Do not take life too seriously—you will never get out of it alive.

– Theodore Roosevelt

playback equipment in Scandinavia. She had no alternative plan. The presentation did not go well.

A solution to such situations is to be aware that all visual equipment is not compatible worldwide. Send a sample of the videos ahead of you to be checked—just to be sure. Always carry an alternative presentation approach you can use without visual projection in case of equipment failure.

WORKING WITH OTHER LANGUAGES

Inexperienced international presenters find themselves trying to speak a little louder—hoping the extra volume will help listeners understand the differences in language. Unfortunately, additional volume won't help much. Working with other languages is a significant challenge for presenters.

A life without surrender is a life without commitment.

– Jerry Rubin

Following are suggestions that will help when you work with other languages:

1. Learn as much as you can about the other language before you arrive. A few key words in that language will help you get along with your new friends.
2. Work through a translator rather than read your presentation in the foreign language.
3. Contact your translator early in your preparation to find out how to prepare your presentation for maximum success in the new language. Translators have usually worked with presenters like you before and can make valuable suggestions that will help you.
4. Keep concepts very simple. Plan one-third less material when you are struggling with the new language than you would use if you were presenting in your own language. Provide copies of material so the translator can become familiar with your presentation.
5. Rehearse with your translator before the presentation. Spend some time with the translator to discover personality nuances and to assess the translator's ability in your language.
6. Articulate your words clearly with a little more volume than usual and with additional space between your words. Use familiar words, where possible.
7. Be patient with your translator. Allow time for the entire translation of each thought.

8. Avoid humor. Humor varies in cultures. What is funny in one language will likely not be so funny in another. Jokes and humor do not translate very well. You will lose a lot of credibility if you insist on using humor in different languages, unless you are sure the humor will work.

9. Don't make any comments in your language you wouldn't make in the foreign language. English speakers who travel internationally often think they can say things in English they would not say in the foreign language. The world is far too international and sophisticated in nature to make that mistake.

In each of us there are places where we have never gone. Only by pressing the limits do you ever find them.

– Dr. Joyce Brothers

Presenting to listeners who speak a language different from yours adds quite a challenge to your presentation. In such situations, keep your presentation clear and simple. Your listeners will appreciate the understanding you bring to their country.

COPING WITH TIME CHANGES AND JET LAG

Time changes and jet lag go together for the experienced presenter who travels a great deal. Experienced presenters adapt to and cope with time changes within the continental United States. That attitude is very important. A presenter who makes excuses about jet lag doesn't get much sympathy from most audiences, so you shouldn't even mention jet lag in such situations. Following are suggestions about how to cope with time changes:

1. Adjust your watch to local time when you arrive. You don't want to miss an appointment.

2. Go to bed according to the time on the clock—not according to your biological clock. You will probably not be sleepy in New York at 11 PM if you come from Los Angeles where the time is 8 PM. However, you will be very sleepy at 6 AM in New York when the time is only 3 AM in Los Angeles. Try to allow five to six hours of sleep on the first night. If you stay a second night, you will have an easier time sleeping according to the clock.

Unrest of spirit is a mark of life.

– Karl Menninger

3. Eat meals according to the local time. You will have to force yourself for the first day or two, but the time will work in your favor after that. Lighter meals work best in the adjustment period. A little snacking may help you get through the adjustment period.

4. Set two wake-up alarms. Most hotels provide reliable alarm clocks in their rooms. That means you can set the alarm clock and also call for a telephone wake-up for the same time. If you carry a small alarm clock with you (which we strongly suggest), you may even set a third alarm.

5. Get into an exercise program. A physically fit body is more likely to respond to time changes than one that is not in shape.

Strength is born in the deep silence of long-suffering hearts; not amid joy.

– Felicia Hemans

International travel provides great time-difference challenges. The time stays relatively constant in North and South America and can be dealt with much like United States domestic travel. However, the pressure of traveling into any new country increases problems with sleeping.

Arriving a day early to an international destination to allow for physiological adjustment is a wise move if your schedule will allow it.

Jet lag and time changes are an expected product of most travel. Even though most adjustments can be made quite easily, the traveler needs to pay attention to keeping rested and alert.

Following are suggestions for adjusting to jet lag for international travel:

1. Arrive a day early so that you can get your body on local time.

2. Avoid exotic international foods in the early stages of your trip.

3. Make yourself get up at a reasonable time (local time) the first morning you are there, especially if you have an extra day to get used to the environment. This procedure works well even if you have to take a short nap in the afternoon.

4. Take controlled naps if you take any naps at all during the early part of your stay. Don't let yourself get a night's sleep in an afternoon nap. Naps are not recommended, even though they sometimes seem to be essential.

5. Keep busy in the early stages of your trip. If you have the luxury of an extra day, use that day for walks or light sightseeing, reading, doing work you take with you, etc. Make yourself work during the day, and sleep during the night.

Biological clocks vary with individuals—and especially with people who are in less than top physical shape. Be wise in what you expect your body to do.

The first and great commandment is, Don't let them scare you.

– Elmer Davis

Don't let yourself get a night's sleep in an afternoon nap.

One traveler who was traveling from the Mountain West in America to Stockholm, Sweden, an eight-hour time change, started his meetings on Monday morning. He arranged to leave Friday morning on his 18-hour trip, plus an 8-hour time change. As a normal traveler, he didn't get much sleep on a full airplane.

He checked into his hotel by 11 AM Saturday morning. He took a two-hour nap. At 1 PM, he went out for a walk and some light lunch. He took a short sight-seeing tour, walked some more, did some preparation for Monday's meetings, ate a light dinner, read, and went to bed about 9:30 PM.

His biological clock woke him up at 4 AM. He read, worked through some preparation until 7 AM, and proceeded with a somewhat normal Sunday. He took a 30-minute nap early in the afternoon. His body wanted three hours, but he could not afford that luxury.

He went to bed at 10 PM and slept until the biological clock went off at 5 AM. He was then reasonably ready to begin his work day, somewhat rested. He was relatively normal in the time schedule by the third day.

The return trip is also difficult and requires the same effort.

Without the element of uncertainty, the bringing off of even the greatest business triumph would be a dull, routine, and eminently unsatisfying affair.

– J. Paul Getty

STAYING COMFORTABLY
AND SAFELY IN HOTELS

Businesspeople who present frequently spend many nights in hotels. Most companies provide middle- to upper-level hotels for their employees. Hotel staying is more than a bed in a strange place. You must be somewhat comfortable in your surroundings. Many hotels provide very comfortable accommodations for businesspeople. Shop around to find the type of lodging that fits your lifestyle.

The art of life lies in a constant readjustment to our surroundings.

– Kakuzo Okakura

The following suggestions will help you as you stay comfortably and safely in domestic and international hotels:

1. Plan to arrive in daylight hours, especially in cities you are visiting for the first time. Early arrival times will allow you to get your bearings in the new environment.

> **New places always look better in the light. You can see what you are doing, where you have been, and where you are going.**

2. Determine how much time you will need to get from your hotel to your place of business in the new city. The hotel employees will be able to tell you about traffic problems the next morning.
3. Determine your mode of travel while you are in the new city. Rental cars may or may not be your best mode of travel because parking and heavy traffic are a problem in large cities. In most cities, taxis and buses will probably be your best means of transportation. Business visits to outlying areas will probably require a rental vehicle.

> **In most cities, taxis and buses will probably be your best means of transportation.**

4. Make guaranteed, late-arrival reservations if any chance exists you will be arriving at the hotel after 6 PM. You will be

responsible to pay for the room if you do not arrive, as a guaranteed reservation room will be held all night for you. You will be asked to leave a credit card number in guaranteeing your reservations.

If you find you cannot arrive as planned, most hotels will respond to a reasonable phone request to cancel— even after 6 PM.

5. Request no-smoking rooms if that is your preference. Most hotels offer no-smoking rooms, and often they offer no-smoking floors. Most hotels work with you in seeing that your request is granted if they can.

6. Check out the safety features in and around each hotel property. Some businesses and hotels are located in areas where safety is a question. Even in the daytime, caution should be exercised in many locations. Stay close to facilities, ask lobby staff for safety tips, and walk in groups where possible.

A traveler can be an easy mark for people who prey on other people. A little attention to safety details can literally save your life.

Following are some additional safety tips for traveling:

1. Keep hotel rooms locked at all times.
2. Locate emergency exits and know how you would evacuate if necessary.
3. Store large sums of cash in hotel safes.
4. Know where your airplane ticket is at all times. Carrying it with you may not be the best arrangement.
5. Order room service if eating alone in a restaurant concerns you.
6. Carry a small flashlight and fresh batteries in your luggage in case of a hotel emergency.
7. Follow hunches as you move around the hotel. If you are alone on an elevator when someone gets on who makes you nervous, step out and wait for another elevator.
8. Tell people where you are going and when you are returning. These people include associates, hotel personnel, and people at home.

9. Stay out of stairwells whenever possible.
10. Carry small bills with you as you shop and eat. Don't flash large amounts of money in public places.
11. Watch your credit card carefully as it is being used. Take the time to replace it in your purse or pocket after each use.

CHAPTER SUMMARY

Being a reasonable person is a key part of being a successful presenter. *Reasonable* means you can adapt to and cope with situations that arise. Taking care of details well in advance will do much to reduce the amount of adapting and coping you will have to do around the presentation.

Traveling in international circles, working with another language, coping with jet lag and time changes, and being comfortable and safe in hotel situations are also important parts of adapting and coping. Taking the specific steps mentioned in this chapter will help you deal with different and unexpected situations.

The presentation is dependent upon taking care of everything around it. You will be more likely to be successful if you will heed the suggestions given in this chapter.

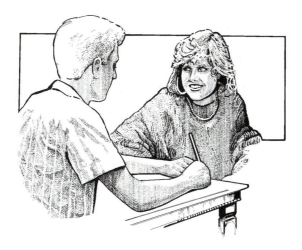

EXERCISES

1. Interview three people who have made presentations in
    international settings. Make a list of the unique situations
    they found. Think about how this list might help you in
    international situations.

2. Interview two persons who have made presentations in a coun-
    try whose people speak a language different from the presenters.
    Specifically ask the following questions:

    a. Did you use an interpreter?
    b. What suggestions do you have about using an
        interpreter?
    c. What surprises did you find in presenting through
        an interpreter?
    d. If you did not use an interpreter, how did you cope with
        the language barrier?

3. Make a list of suggestions to give to someone who has a particu-
    larly difficult time adjusting to and coping with surprises or
    difficult situations.

4. Speak with three people who travel extensively and ask them
    about their experiences concerning safety and comfort in hotel
    situations. List five steps you might take to ensure comfort and
    safety for yourself as you travel.